BLACK & DECKER®
HOME IMPROVEMENT LIBRARY™

Advanced Deck Building

COWLES
Creative Publishing

A Division of Cowles Enthusiast Media, Inc.

Contents

Copyright © 1996
Cowles Creative Publishing, Inc.
Formerly Cy DeCosse Incorporated
5900 Green Oak Drive
Minnetonka, Minnesota 55343
1-800-328-3895
All rights reserved
Printed in U.S.A.

Books available in this series:
*Everyday Home Repairs, Decorating
With Paint & Wallcovering, Carpentry:
Tools • Shelves • Walls • Doors, Kitchen
Remodeling, Building Decks, Home Plumbing
Projects & Repairs, Basic Wiring & Electrical
Repairs, Workshop Tips & Techniques,
Advanced Home Wiring, Carpentry:
Remodeling, Landscape Design &
Construction, Bathroom Remodeling, Built-in
Projects for the Home, Kitchen & Bathroom
Ideas, Refinishing & Finishing Wood,
Exterior Home Repairs & Improvements,
Home Masonry Repairs & Projects, Building
Porches & Patios, Deck & Landscape
Ideas, Flooring Projects & Techniques*

Library of Congress
Cataloging-in-Publication Data

Advanced deck building.
p. cm.—(Black & Decker home
improvement library)
Includes index.
ISBN 0-86573-666-9 (hardcover).
ISBN 0-86573-661-8 (softcover).
1. Decks (Architecture, Domestic)—Design
and construction.
I. Cowles Creative Publishing.
II. Series.
TH4970.A38 1997
690'.893—dc21   96-48313

COWLES
Creative Publishing
A Division of Cowles Enthusiast Media, Inc.

President/COO: Nino Tarantino
Executive V.P./Editor-in-Chief:
  William B. Jones

Created by: The Editors of Cowles
Creative Publishing, Inc., in cooperation
with Black & Decker. ● **BLACK&DECKER** is a
trademark of the Black & Decker
Corporation and is used under license.

Executive Editor: Paul Currie
Editorial Director: Mark Johanson
Managing Editor: Kristen Olson
Associate Creative Director: Tim Himsel
Lead Art Director: John Hermansen
Art Director: Gina Seeling
Project Manager: Lori Holmberg
Senior Editor: Bryan Trandem
Editor & Lead Researcher: Joel Schmarje
Editor & Technical Artist: Jon Simpson
Editor: Carol Harvatin
Editorial Assistant: Andrew Sweet
Senior Technical Production Editor:
  Gary Sandin
Technical Production Editors: Dan Cary,
  Greg Pluth
Copy Editor: Janice Cauley

Vice President of Photography &
  Production: Jim Bindas
Production Managers: Kim Gerber,
  Gretchen Gundersen
Shop Supervisor: Phil Juntti
Lead Set Builder: John Nadeau
Set Builders: Troy Johnson, Rob Johnstone
Production Staff: Tom Hoops, Guy
  Messenger, Mike Schauer, Brent Thomas,
  Kay Wethern
Studio Services Manager: Marcia Chambers
Photo Services Coordinator: Cheryl Neisen
Lead Photographer: Rex Irmen
Photographer's Assistant: Andria Moldzio
Photographers: Rebecca Schmitt,
  Greg Wallace
Contributing Photography: Archadeck,
  California Redwood Association, Lindal
  Cedar Homes, Milt Charno & Associates,
  Osmose Wood Preserving, Western
  Wood Products Association, Wolman
  Wood Care Products
Contributing Manufacturers: USP Kant-
  Sag•Silver

COWLES
Enthusiast Media

President/COO: Philip L. Penny

Deck Plans Produced in Conjunction with:
  Homestyles; Milt Charno & Associates, Inc.

Printed on American paper by:
  Quebecor Printing
  99 98 97 96 / 5 4 3 2 1

Introduction

In the last few decades, hundreds of thousands of wood decks have been built in backyards across this continent. Most of these decks serve their practical function admirably, providing a limited amount of space in which to comfortably enjoy outdoor living. But few of these decks genuinely enhance the look of the home and surrounding landscape, and of those that succeed on this level, nearly all are built by landscape professionals at prodigious cost.

Advanced Deck Building is the first book to show you how to design and build your own designer deck. In it, you'll learn how to create the kind of unique features usually found only in decks designed and built by professionals: distinctive low-profile decks; curved decks with sweeping railings; spacious multilevel decks; towering decks built on steep slopes; and polygon-shaped decks with angled sides. You'll also learn how to add a stairway with a landing and how to build unique deck railings. And, as a special bonus, we have included a section containing a dozen stunning, advanced deck plans, created by professional deck designers. You can use these 12 plans for ideas as you design your own deck, or you can order complete detailed blueprints for any of the decks featured.

This book offers an advanced course in deck design and construction. Because we presume that readers already have some knowledge of deck construction, beginning do-it-yourselfers should use this book only in conjunction with one or more good books on basic deck-building skills, such as *Building Decks* from the Black & Decker® Home Improvement Library™.

Advanced Deck Building opens with several pages of color photos that demonstrate how a sophisticated deck design can enhance your outdoor living space. Next, you'll find a chapter on "Design & Planning," showing you how to find deck ideas, develop those ideas into a workable plan, work with building officials, and incorporate advanced features into your deck.

The heart of the book is the next chapter, "Advanced Techniques," where you'll learn specific techniques and methods used by professionals to create decks with unique shapes and features.

A Gallery of Distinctive Decks

With decks, the difference between serviceable and sensational can be very slight. Often, it takes only one or two unique features to make an otherwise ordinary deck stand out from the crowd. A curved platform, a well-placed angle, a decorative railing—there are many special design features employed by professional deck designers to turn decks into distinctive structures. In the following pages, you'll find many examples of ways the professionals use advanced features to improve deck appearance and add functions that make sense in their setting and for their owners.

Use the following pages to gain inspiration and information—any do-it-yourselfer with patience and moderate tool skills can design and build a professional-quality deck that is custom-fitted to specific tastes and needs.

Provide a graceful alternative to a plain patio: In this landscape, the low-profile, curved deck platforms create the visual effect of a raised living area, adding new textures and dimensions to a plain, flat patio. Decoration is also used to enhance the effect, as the wood benches and clay flowerpots create an atmosphere that is relaxed yet slightly formal.

Frame a view—the sweeping lines and rounded profile of this curved deck reach out into a wooded landscape toward an inviting lake. The effect, together with the use of a unique cable-and-post railing structure, enhances the panoramic view from the house.

(continued next page)

Increase living space. This wraparound deck extends outdoor living space and provides a tranquil balcony from which to enjoy the wooded surroundings. The pattern of the baluster railing echoes the strong vertical lines of the A-frame house and the tall trees that surround the home, while evergreen shrubs and shredded bark ground cover provide a visual transition between the home and the landscape.

Make attractive transitions between outdoor and indoor living spaces. This rectangular deck (right) is nestled into the hillside of a sloped lot. A grand staircase echoing the design of the deck bridges the space between deck and home. The net effect is that of an exterior "foyer" between the street and front door.

Display custom craftsmanship.
In this large, multilevel deck (right), the angled construction allowed the builder to preserve the yard's natural setting by working around mature trees. In addition, the built-in benches help enclose the deck and are constructed so the pattern formed by the surface boards contrasts with that of the decking boards. The overall effect is a one-of-a-kind structure custom-made for the space it occupies.

Support multiple activities
by building a deck with multiple levels. Multilevel decks add visual interest to a yard and create distinct areas that can serve different uses. In this example, patio doors open onto an expansive upper deck platform that is ideal for entertaining, while a smaller lower level with built-in benches creates an intimate conversation area. A stairway forms a gradual transition that separates the two spaces without isolating them.

Create a sense of harmony in your backyard landscape. A cherished tree becomes the focal point of this deck design, joining forces with an expansive overhead arbor to provide shelter and shade. Successfully blending nature into a deck design provides strong visual interest and a sense of peaceful coexistence in this low-profile redwood deck.

Showcase a social centerpiece. The fire pit framed into this redwood deck provides a dramatic focal point for the sitting area. When positioned a safe distance away from permanent structures and designed with raised walls and fireproof materials, a fire pit creates a safe, cozy conversation corner, ideal for use on cool evenings.

Enhance outdoor recreation with a deck that is designed for activity. This expansive, intricate deck (left) surrounds an above-ground swimming pool to create a sunning deck for the homeowners. A sturdy railing maintains privacy and complies with local Codes for yards that contain water features.

Design & Planning

A building permit is granted after an official from the building inspections department has reviewed and approved your deck plans. Consulting a building official early in the planning process can help ensure that the approval process is a smooth one.

Planning Your Project

When building a deck, the importance of planning cannot be overemphasized. Poor planning almost always leads to frustration and disappointment, but good planning helps ensure that your new deck will be an attractive, functional space that adds value to your home.

Careful planning helps guarantee that your deck will meet your needs—both aesthetically and functionally. Good planning also makes for a trouble-free construction process.

The planning process begins with gathering raw ideas and ends with a building official granting you a permit to begin work. Between these steps,

you'll need to develop your initial idea into a detailed plan drawing, review the basics of deck construction, and learn how to integrate advanced features into your deck.

In this section you will find information on:
• Where to Find Deck Ideas (page 15)
• Developing Your Deck Plan (pages 16 to 17)
• Reviewing the Basics (pages 18 to 19)
• Advanced Deck Features (pages 20 to 25)
• Working with Building Officials (pages 26 to 27)
• Understanding Loads (pages 28 to 29)
• Advanced Construction Tips (pages 30 to 31)

Where to Find Deck Ideas

Purchased deck plans, sales literature, and home improvement magazines are good sources of ideas. Deck plans are widely available, but you may need to revise them extensively to make them work for your building site. Sales literature from lumber suppliers and hardware manufacturers often features photos and plan drawings of elaborate decks, which you can use to develop your own design.

Books on outdoor construction techniques, such as *Building Decks* and *Building Porches & Patios* from the Black & Decker® Home Improvement Library™, can provide you with deck ideas. They can also give you a valuable refresher course on basic construction methods. In addition, the last chapter of *Advanced Deck Building* includes over a dozen advanced deck plans you may be able to use.

Personal scouting is perhaps the best source of ideas. Whenever you go out for a drive or walk, keep an eye open for unique, attractive decks. Carry a camera to photograph construction details—after getting the consent of the property owner.

Developing Your Deck Plan

Computer software makes the deck design process simpler. These programs range from relatively inexpensive but full-featured software designed for the do-it-yourself consumer (above), to specialized CAD software used mostly by design professionals. Some consumer software programs include a "library" of stock deck designs that you can revise to suit your needs.

Once you have a rough idea of what you want your deck to look like, you'll need to develop the concept into a workable plan. Especially for complicated, elaborate decks, it is crucial that you have detailed plan drawings to help organize and direct your work. Good plans also make it possible to create an accurate materials list. In addition, your building inspector will insist on seeing plan drawings before granting you a work permit.

One surefire method is to hire a landscape designer to develop a detailed deck blueprint, but this process is often expensive and is less rewarding than creating your own design. With careful, thoughtful work, you can develop a plan tailored exactly to your needs, and save money in the process.

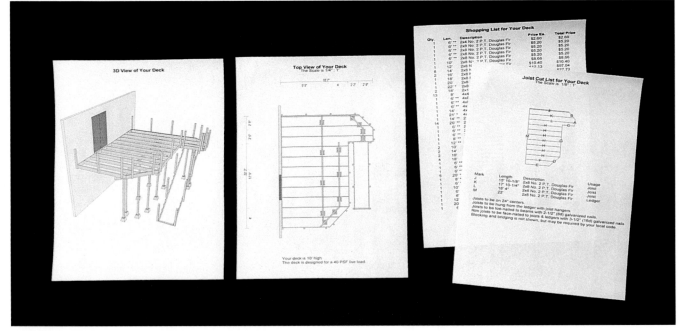

Computer printouts generated by deck-design software provide three-dimensional views of finished deck designs (left), detailed structural drawings (center), and a complete list of the materials needed (right). Some design programs can even print out contracts and forms, such as building permit applications.

Tips for Developing a Deck Plan

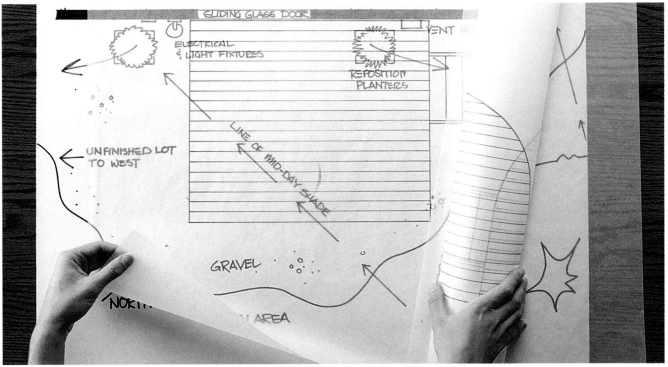

Use tracing paper to sketch different deck layouts. Then, test your ideas by overlaying the deck sketches onto a drawing of your building site. Make sure to consider sun patterns and the locations of existing landscape features when developing a deck plan.

Adapt an existing deck plan, either borrowed from a book or magazine, or purchased in blueprint form. Tracing paper, pens, and measuring tools are all you need to revise an existing deck plan.

Use drafting tools and graph paper if you are creating a deck plan from scratch. Use a generous scale, such as 1" equals 1 ft., that allows you to illustrate the deck in fine detail. Remember to create both overhead plan drawings and side elevation drawings of your project.

Reviewing the Basics

This book assumes the reader already has some experience or knowledge of basic deck-building techniques. Before attempting an elaborate, complicated deck, make sure you have a full grasp of the basic deck-building skills, as summarized in the step-by-step overview shown here. If you do not fully understand each of these steps, review one or more books on deck construction, including *Building Decks,* the book from which these photographs are taken. Once you are comfortable with the principles of building a simple rectangular deck, it will be easier to use the advanced techniques in this book.

1 Install a ledger to anchor the deck to the house and to serve as a reference for laying out locations for footings. The standard method for laying out footings is with batterboards and mason's strings.

4 Attach metal joist hangers to the ledger and rim joist, then hang the remaining joists. On a simple deck, joists should be spaced 16" on center if the decking boards will be attached perpendicular to the joists; 12" on center if they will be laid diagonally.

5 Attach the decking boards, and use a circular saw to trim the ends flush with the outside joists and rim joist. For a more attractive appearance, you can cover the rim joist and outside joists with redwood or cedar facing boards.

2 Pour concrete post footings and install metal post anchors. Set and brace the posts, then attach them to the post anchors and mark the posts to show where the beam will be attached.

3 Attach the beam to the posts, then install the outside joists and rim joist.

6 Build a stairway to provide a pathway between the yard and deck. The position you choose for the stairway helps determine how traffic will cross your deck.

7 Install a railing around the deck and stairway. A railing adds a decorative touch and is required for any deck that is more than 30" above the ground.

Advanced Deck Features

On the following pages you will see illustrations of several decks, each containing several advanced features that are usually found only on elaborate decks designed and built by professionals.

Incorporating these features into a deck you design and build yourself is not as difficult as you might imagine. First, you'll need a good understanding of basic deck-building skills, as outlined on the previous pages. There are many good books on deck-building techniques which can help you brush up on your skills.

Once you are confident of your basic skills, you will need to learn a few special construction methods. These techniques are noted on the following few pages, and are described in full detail in the next chapter—"Advanced Techniques."

Hot tubs installed on a deck must have extra beams and closely spaced joists to support the extra weight. See pages 80 to 83.

Stairway railings must be installed on any stairway with more than two steps, and should have grippable handrails. See pages 92 to 93.

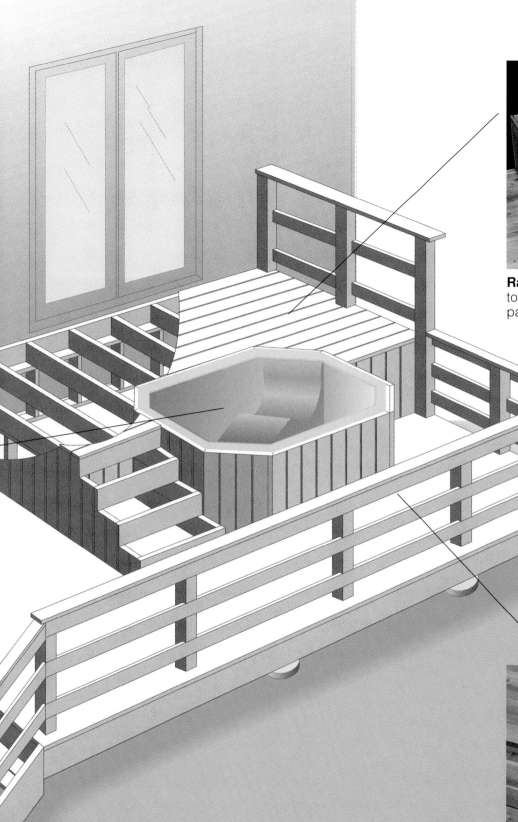

Raised platforms are often used to partially enclose a hot tub. See pages 80 to 83.

Horizontal railings blend well with modern house styles. The railing can be built by framing posts into the deck structure, then mortising the rails into the posts for improved strength. See page 88.

21

Low-profile decks feature beams that rest directly on concrete footings instead of posts. See pages 34 to 37.

Insets are an effective way to build a deck around your favorite landscape features. See pages 76 to 79.

Curved railings rely on the use of geometry and special layout and construction techniques to create the curved top rail and cap rail. See pages 94 to 97.

Curved decks are usually built by cutting joists to a circular outline, then attaching a curved rim joist. See pages 70 to 75.

Wall-style railings make a deck more private and allow it to visually blend in with the house. See pages 90 to 91.

Multilevel decks can share the same row of posts along the overlapping sides. See pages 38 to 45.

Vertical railings use balusters attached to rails that are mortised into the posts, providing greater strength and a more finished appearance. See pages 86 to 88.

Decorative treatments like lattice panels can dress up or conceal the area below a deck. See pages 98 to 101.

Landings are required whenever a deck stairway has 12 or more steps. See pages 46 to 55.

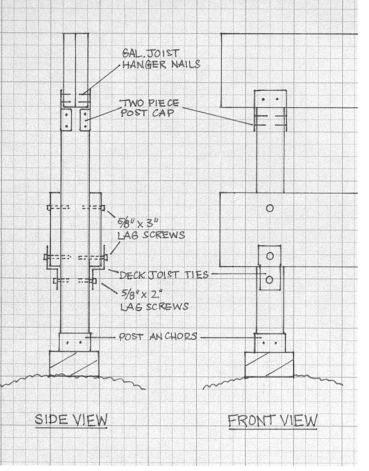

GAL. JOIST HANGER NAILS

TWO PIECE POST CAP

5/8" x 3" LAG SCREWS

DECK JOIST TIES

5/8" x 2" LAG SCREWS

POST ANCHORS

SIDE VIEW   FRONT VIEW

Draw detailed illustrations of the joinery methods you plan to use on all structural members of your deck. Your building official will want to see details on post-footing connections, post-beam joints, beam-joist joints, and ledger connections.

Working with Building Officials

In most regions, you must have your plans reviewed and approved by a building official if your deck is attached to a permanent structure, or if it is more than 30" high. The building official makes sure that your planned deck meets Building Code requirements for safe construction.

These pages show some of the most common Code requirements for decks. But before you design your project, check with the building inspection division of your city office, since Code regulations can vary from area to area. A valuable source of planning information, the building official may provide you with a free information sheet outlining the relevant requirements.

Once you have completed plans for your deck, return to the building inspections office and have the official review them. If your plans meet Code, you will be issued a building permit, usually for a small fee. Regulations may require that a field inspector review the deck at specified stages in the building process. If so, make sure to comply with the review schedule.

Plan-approval Checklist

When the building official reviews your deck plans, he or she will look for the following details. Make sure your plan drawings include this information when you visit the building inspection office to apply for a building permit.

- Overall size of the deck.
- Position of the deck relative to buildings and property lines. The deck must be set back at least 5 ft. from neighboring property.
- Location of all beams and posts.
- Size and on-center (OC) spacing of joists.
- Thickness of decking boards.
- Height of deck above the ground.
- Detailed drawings of joinery methods for all structural members of the deck.
- Type of soil that will support the concrete post footings: sand, gravel, or clay.
- Species of wood you will be using.
- Types of metal connectors and other hardware you plan to use when constructing your deck.

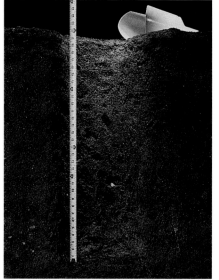

Footing diameter and depth is determined by your building official, based on the estimated load of the deck and on the composition of your soil. In regions with cold winters, footings must extend below the frost line. Minimum diameter for concrete footings is 8".

Tips for Working with Building Officials

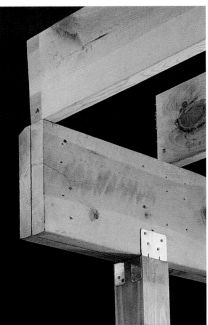

Metal flashings must be used to prevent moisture from penetrating between the ledger and the wall.

Beams may overhang posts by no more than 1 ft. Wherever possible, beams should rest on top of posts, secured with metal post-beam caps.

Engineered beams, such as a laminated wood product or steel girder, should be used on decks with very long joist spans, where standard dimension lumber is not adequate for the load.

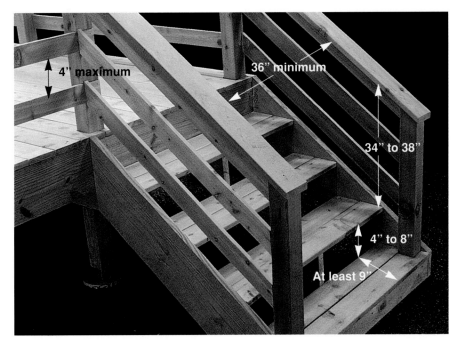

4" maximum

36" minimum

34" to 38"

4" to 8"

At least 9"

Railings are required for any deck more than 30" above the ground; railings must be at least 36" in height, and the bottom rail must be positioned so there is no more than 6" of open space below it. Vertical balusters can have no more than 4" between them.

Stairs must be at least 36" wide. Vertical step risers must be between 4" and 8", and treads must have a horizontal run of at least 9". A single staircase can have no more than 12 steps; for longer runs, two staircases are required, separated by a landing. Stair railings should be 34" to 38" above the noses of the step treads, and there should be no more than 6" of space between the bottom rail and the steps. The space between the rails or balusters should be no more than 4".

Understanding Loads

The supporting structural members of a deck—the posts, beams, and joists—must be sturdy enough to easily support the heaviest anticipated load on the deck. They must not only carry the substantial weight of the surface decking and railings, but also the weight of people, deck furnishings, and, in some climates, snow.

The charts and diagrams shown here will help you plan a deck so the size and spacing of the structural members are sufficient to support the load, assuming normal use. These recommendations are followed in most regions, but you should still check with your local building official for regulations that are unique to your area. In cases where the deck will support a hot tub or pool, you must consult your local building inspections office for load guidelines.

When choosing lumber for the structural members of your deck, select the diagram below that best matches your deck design, then follow the advice for applying the charts on the opposite page. Since different species of wood have different strength, make sure to use the entries that match the type of lumber sold by your building center. When selecting the size for concrete footings, make sure to consider the composition of your soil; dense soils require footings with a larger diameter.

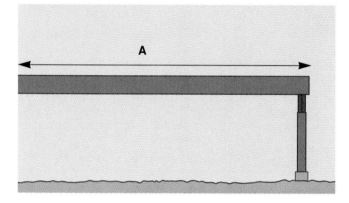

Corner-post deck: Using Chart 1, determine the proper size for your joists, based on the on-center (OC) spacing between joists and the overall length, or span, of the joists (A). For example, if you will be using southern pine joists to span a 12-ft. distance, you can use 2 × 8 lumber spaced no more than 16" apart, or 2 × 10 lumber spaced no more than 24" apart. Once you have determined allowable joist sizes, use Chart 2 to determine an appropriate beam size, post spacing, and footing size for your deck.

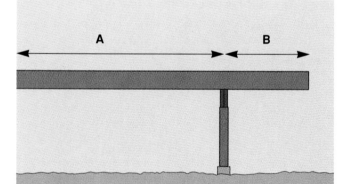

Cantilevered deck: Use the distance from the ledger to the beam (A) to determine minimum joist size, and use A + (2 × B) when choosing beam and footing sizes. For example, if your deck measures 9 ft. from ledger to beam, with an additional 3-ft. cantilevered overhang, use 9 ft. to choose a joist size from Chart 1 (2 × 6 southern pine joists spaced 16" apart, or 2 × 8 joists spaced 24" apart). Then, use A + (2 × B), or 15 ft., to find an appropriate beam size, post spacing, and footing size from Chart 2. NOTE: If your deck cantilevers more than 18" beyond the support beam, add 1" to the recommended diameter for footings.

Multiple-beam deck: Use distance A or B, whichever is larger, when determining joist size from Chart 1. For example, if your deck measures 8 ft. to beam #1 and another 4 ft. to beam #2, you can use 2 × 6 southern pine joists. Referring to chart 2, use the total distance A + B to determine the size of beam #1, the spacing for the posts, and the size of the footings. Use joist length B to determine the size of beam #2, the post spacing, and footing size. For example, with an overall span of 12 ft. (8 ft. to the first beam, 4 ft. to the second), beam #1 could be made from two southern pine 2 × 8s; beam #2, from two 2 × 6s.

Chart 1

Size	Southern Pine 12" OC	Southern Pine 16" OC	Southern Pine 24" OC	Ponderosa Pine 12" OC	Ponderosa Pine 16" OC	Ponderosa Pine 24" OC	Western Cedar 12" OC	Western Cedar 16" OC	Western Cedar 24" OC
2 × 6	10 ft. 9"	9 ft. 9"	8 ft. 6"	9 ft. 2"	8 ft. 4"	7 ft. 0"	9 ft. 2"	8 ft. 4"	7 ft. 3"
2 × 8	14 ft. 2"	12 ft. 10"	11 ft. 0"	12 ft. 1"	10 ft. 10"	8 ft. 10"	12 ft. 1"	11 ft. 0"	9 ft. 2"
2 × 10	18 ft. 0"	16 ft. 1"	13 ft. 5"	15 ft. 4"	13 ft. 3"	10 ft. 10"	15 ft. 5"	13 ft. 9"	11 ft. 3"
2 × 12	21 ft. 9"	19 ft. 0"	15 ft. 4"	17 ft. 9"	15 ft. 5"	12 ft. 7"	18 ft. 5"	16 ft. 0"	13 ft. 0"

Chart 2

Footing cells list three values in the order Clay, Sand, Gravel.

Joist Length		Post Spacing 4'	5'	6'	7'	8'	9'	10'	11'	12'
6'	Southern Pine Beam	1–2×6	1–2×6	1–2×6	2–2×6	2–2×6	2–2×6	2–2×8	2–2×8	2–2×10
	Ponderosa Pine Beam	1–2×6	1–2×6	1–2×8	2–2×8	2–2×8	2–2×8	2–2×10	2–2×10	2–2×12
	Corner Footing	6 5 4	7 6 5	7 6 5	8 7 6	9 7 6	9 7 6	10 8 7	10 8 7	10 9 7
	Intermediate Footing	9 8 7	10 8 7	10 9 7	11 9 8	12 10 9	13 10 9	14 11 10	14 12 10	15 12 10
7'	Southern Pine Beam	1–2×6	1–2×6	1–2×6	2–2×6	2–2×6	2–2×8	2–2×8	2–2×10	2–2×10
	Ponderosa Pine Beam	1–2×6	1–2×6	1–2×8	2–2×8	2–2×8	2–2×10	2–2×10	2–2×10	2–2×12
	Corner Footing	7 5 5	7 6 5	8 7 6	9 7 6	9 8 7	10 8 7	10 8 7	11 9 8	11 9 8
	Intermediate Footing	9 8 7	10 8 7	11 9 8	12 10 9	13 11 9	14 11 10	15 12 10	15 13 11	16 13 11
8'	Southern Pine Beam	1–2×6	1–2×6	2–2×6	2–2×6	2–2×8	2–2×8	2–2×8	2–2×10	2–2×10
	Ponderosa Pine Beam	1–2×6	2–2×6	2–2×8	2–2×8	2–2×8	2–2×10	2–2×10	2–2×10	3–2×10
	Corner Footing	7 6 5	8 6 6	9 7 6	9 8 7	10 8 7	10 8 7	11 9 8	11 9 8	12 10 9
	Intermediate Footing	10 8 7	11 9 8	12 10 9	13 11 9	14 11 10	15 12 10	16 13 11	16 13 12	17 14 12
9'	Southern Pine Beam	1–2×6	1–2×6	2–2×6	2–2×6	2–2×8	2–2×8	2–2×8	2–2×10	2–2×12
	Ponderosa Pine Beam	1–2×6	2–2×6	2–2×8	2–2×8	2–2×10	2–2×10	2–2×10	3–2×10	3–2×10
	Corner Footing	7 6 5	8 7 6	9 7 6	10 8 7	10 9 7	11 9 8	12 10 8	12 10 9	13 10 9
	Intermediate Footing	10 9 7	12 10 8	13 10 9	14 11 10	15 12 10	16 13 11	17 14 12	17 14 12	18 15 13
10'	Southern Pine Beam	1–2×6	1–2×6	2–2×6	2–2×6	2–2×8	2–2×8	2–2×10	2–2×10	2–2×12
	Ponderosa Pine Beam	1–2×6	1–2×6	2–2×8	2–2×8	2–2×10	2–2×10	2–2×12	3–2×10	3–2×12
	Corner Footing	8 6 6	9 7 6	10 8 7	10 8 7	11 9 8	12 10 8	12 10 9	13 11 9	14 11 10
	Intermediate Footing	11 9 8	12 10 9	14 11 10	15 12 10	16 13 11	17 14 12	17 14 12	18 15 13	19 16 14
11'	Southern Pine Beam	1–2×6	2–2×6	2–2×6	2–2×8	2–2×8	2–2×10	2–2×10	2–2×12	2–2×12
	Ponderosa Pine Beam	2–2×6	2–2×6	2–2×8	2–2×8	2–2×10	2–2×12	2–2×12	3–2×10	3–2×12
	Corner Footing	8 7 6	9 7 6	10 8 7	11 9 8	12 9 8	12 10 9	13 11 9	14 11 10	14 12 10
	Intermediate Footing	12 9 8	13 11 9	14 12 10	15 12 10	16 13 11	17 14 12	17 14 12	18 15 13	19 16 14
12'	Southern Pine Beam	1–2×6	2–2×6	2–2×6	2–2×8	2–2×8	2–2×10	2–2×10	2–2×12	3–2×10
	Ponderosa Pine Beam	2–2×6	2–2×6	2–2×8	2–2×10	2–2×10	2–2×12	2–2×12	3–2×10	3–2×12
	Corner Footing	9 7 6	10 8 7	10 9 7	11 9 8	12 10 9	13 10 9	14 11 10	14 12 10	15 12 10
	Intermediate Footing	12 10 9	14 11 10	15 12 10	16 13 11	17 14 12	18 15 13	19 16 14	20 16 14	21 17 15
13'	Southern Pine Beam	1–2×6	2–2×6	2–2×6	2–2×8	2–2×8	2–2×10	2–2×10	2–2×12	3–2×10
	Ponderosa Pine Beam	2–2×6	2–2×6	2–2×8	2–2×10	2–2×12	2–2×12	2–2×12	3–2×12	3–2×12
	Corner Footing	9 7 6	10 8 7	11 9 8	12 10 8	13 10 9	13 11 9	14 12 10	15 12 10	15 13 11
	Intermediate Footing	13 10 9	14 12 10	15 13 11	17 14 12	18 15 13	19 15 13	20 16 14	21 17 15	22 18 15
14'	Southern Pine Beam	1–2×6	2–2×6	2–2×6	2–2×8	2–2×10	2–2×10	2–2×12	3–2×10	3–2×12
	Ponderosa Pine Beam	2–2×6	2–2×8	2–2×8	2–2×10	2–2×12	3–2×10	3–2×12	3–2×12	Eng Bm
	Corner Footing	9 8 7	10 8 7	11 9 8	12 10 9	13 11 9	14 11 10	15 12 10	15 13 11	16 13 11
	Intermediate Footing	13 11 9	15 12 10	16 13 11	17 14 12	18 15 13	20 16 14	21 17 15	22 18 15	23 18 16
15'	Southern Pine Beam	2–2×6	2–2×6	2–2×8	2–2×8	2–2×10	2–2×12	2–2×12	3–2×10	3–2×12
	Ponderosa Pine Beam	2–2×6	2–2×8	2–2×8	2–2×10	3–2×10	3–2×10	3–2×12	3–2×12	Eng Bm
	Corner Footing	10 8 7	11 9 8	12 10 8	13 10 9	14 11 10	14 12 10	15 12 11	16 13 11	17 14 12
	Intermediate Footing	14 11 10	15 12 11	17 14 12	18 15 13	19 16 14	20 17 14	21 17 15	22 18 16	23 19 17

KEY:

	Clay	Sand	Gravel
	10	8	7
	14	11	10

KEY: Clay Sand Gravel

29

Deck layout traditionally is done with batterboards and strings (page18), but some situations require different layout methods. For angled decks, the board template method (left) described on pages 66 to 67 is easier than batterboards. For a very high deck, or one built on a steep slope (right), the layout is often done by constructing the outer framework first, then elevating it with a temporary wall to find the exact location for footings and posts (pages 56 to 61).

Advanced Construction Tips

The step-by-step overview shown on pages 18 to 19 outlines the basic steps of deck construction, but more complicated decks require special materials and techniques, like those shown here. If you're building an angled deck, for instance, it is easier to do the basic on-site layout using a board template rather than strings and batterboards. And for a deck with many angles, a speed square helps when marking and cutting lumber.

Whenever possible, build your deck so the beams rest on top of the posts—an arrangement that is stronger than attaching beam timbers to the sides of posts with lag screws.

Post cross-bracing helps stabilize a deck platform, and may be required for raised four-post decks and for stairway landings. For best results, install braces diagonally between support posts.

Cross blocks

Cross blocks between joists help stabilize decks that have very long joist spans. Cross braces are also recommended when constructing a curved deck.

Post-beam caps allow you to rest beams on top of posts. This method provides better support than sandwiching the beam timbers around the posts with lag screws. Two types of post-beam caps are widely available: a single piece cap (left) for use when the beam is the same width as the posts, and an adjustable two-piece cap (right) which can be used when the beam and the posts are not the same width.

Post anchors elevate the bottoms of posts above the footing, helping prevent rot. The post rests on a metal pedestal that fits over a J-bolt embedded in the footing. Once the post is set in place, a nut is screwed onto the J-bolt, the metal flange is bent up against the post, and the post anchor is secured to the post with nails.

How to Build a Beam Using Dimension Lumber

1 Cut the beam timbers to size. Sight along the boards to check for crowning, then position the timbers so the crowns are facing the same direction. Nail the timbers together at the ends, using galvanized 16d nails.

2 Turn the beam on edge, and where the timbers are not flush, toenail the higher board down into the lower one so the edges are forced into alignment. If necessary, use clamps to draw the boards into alignment. Facenail the timbers together with rows of 16d nails spaced about 16" apart.

3 Attach post-beam caps to the outside posts, but leave the caps loose on inside posts. Position the beam in the caps, with the crowned edge up. Check for gaps at the inside posts, and shim under the post-beam caps, if necessary. Secure the beam to the caps and posts with joist-hanger nails.

31

Advanced Techniques

Beams for a low-profile deck often rest directly on concrete footings, with no posts. Because low-profile decks may require 2 × 8 or 2 × 6 joists, an intermediate beam may be required to provide adequate support for these narrower joists. At each end of the last beam, the outside timber is 1½" longer than the inside timber, creating a recess where the end of the rim joist will fit.

Building Low-profile Decks

Building a deck that sits very close to the ground generally is easier than constructing a very high deck, but low-profile situations do require some design modifications. If the deck is extremely low (8" to 12" high), it is best to rest the beams directly on concrete footings, since posts are not practical. The joists usually are hung on the faces of the beams rather than resting on top of the beams; cantilever designs are rarely used. Since the ledger is mounted so low on the house, it may need to be anchored to the foundation wall rather than to the rim joist on your house (right).

A deck that is more than 12" above the ground should have at least one step, either box-frame style, or suspended from the deck.

Masonry sleeves are used to attach a ledger to a masonry foundation. Drill 3"-deep guide holes for the sleeves, using a ⅝" masonry bit, then drive sleeves for ⅜"-diameter lag screws into the holes. Position the ledger, then attach it with lag screws driven through the ledgers and into the masonry sleeves.

Support Options

Direct-bearing hardware is used to secure beams when the deck is very low to the ground. Carefully set the footing forms so the tops are at the planned height, then pour concrete and set the hardware into the wet concrete. Use layout strings to ensure that the hardware is aligned correctly.

Posts and post-beam caps can be used if the full deck height is more than 18". Any posts less than 9" tall are prone to splitting.

Step Options

Box-frame step is a simple platform constructed from dimension lumber and covered with decking boards. Box-frame steps are best suited to mild climates where there is little chance the step will be heaved by frost. See page 37.

Suspended step is hung from the underside of the deck. The step is constructed with joists attached to the lower portions of the deck joists. Suspended steps are a good option in cold-weather climates, where box-frame steps are susceptible to frost heaving. However, this method cannot be used if the step joists run perpendicular to the deck joists. See page 37.

How to Build a Low-profile Deck

1 Install the ledger, then lay out and dig footings. If beams will rest directly on footings, use tube forms. Raise the tubes to the proper height and check them for plumb as you pour the concrete. Smooth off the surfaces of the footings, and insert direct-bearing hardware while the concrete is still wet, using layout strings to ensure that the hardware is aligned correctly.

2 Construct beams (page 31), then position the beams in the direct-bearing hardware. Drill pilot holes and use 3½" lag bolts to secure the beam to the hardware. Mark joist locations on the faces of the beams, then install joist hangers.

3 Cut and install all joists, attaching them with joist-hanger nails. Complete your deck, using standard deck-building techniques. Install a box-frame or suspended step, if desired (page opposite).

How to Build a Box-frame Step

1 Construct a rectangular frame for the step, using dimension lumber (2 × 6 lumber is standard), joining the pieces with deck screws. The step must be at least 36" wide and 9" deep. Cut cross blocks and install them inside the frame, spaced every 16".

2 Dig a flat-bottomed trench where the step will rest, about 4" deep. Fill the trench with compactible gravel, and pack with a tamper. Set the step in position, then measure and attach deck boards to form the tread of the step.

How to Build a Suspended Step

1 Screw 2 × 4 furring strips against one side of the deck joists where the step joists will be installed. These strips provide an offset so the step joists will not conflict with the joist hangers attached to the beam. Use a reciprocating saw to make 1½"-wide notches in the rim joist adjacent to the furring strips. NOTE: To maintain adequate structural strength, notches in the joists should be no more than 1½" deep.

2 Measure and cut step joists, allowing about 3 ft. of nailing surface inside the deck frame, and 9" or more of exposed tread. Make sure the step joists are level with one another, then attach them to the deck joists with deck screws. Cut and attach deck boards to the tread area of the step.

Constructing Multilevel Decks

A multilevel deck has obvious advantages, but many do-it-yourselfers are wary of building such a deck, feeling that it is too complex. In reality, however, a multilevel deck is nothing more than two or more adjacent deck platforms set at different heights. You can build a multilevel deck with the same simple construction techniques used to build a standard deck—with one exception: For efficiency, multilevel decks usually are designed so the platforms share a single support beam on the side where they meet. For this reason, it is essential that the shared posts and beams be sturdy enough to carry the load of both platforms.

Except for the shared beam, the separate platforms on a multilevel deck are independent and can use different construction methods. For example, the upper level might use a corner-post design with decking boards installed perpendicular to the joists, while the lower level might use a curved cantilever design with decking laid at an angle. If your time and budget are limited, you can build your deck in phases, completing one platform at a time at your convenience.

Remember to include railings (pages 84 to 97) and stairs (pages 46 to 55) where needed. Any deck platform more than 30" above the ground—or above a lower deck platform—requires a railing.

Different support methods can be used in the same multilevel deck. In the deck shown here, the top platform is supported by a beam resting on top of posts, while the lower platform is supported by 2 × 12 beam timbers sandwiched around the posts. The opposite side of the lower platform might use yet another support method, such as a set-back beam supporting cantilevered joists.

Design Options

The shared beam method has one beam supporting both platforms where they overlap. The upper platform rests directly on the beam, while the lower hangs from the face of the beam. This method is an economical choice, since only one beam is required, and it is well suited for relatively flat building sites where the deck levels are close together. See pages 40 to 41.

The shared post method has two beams supported by the same row of posts. The top platform is supported by a beam resting on top of the posts, while the beam for the lower platform is built from 2 × 12 timbers sandwiched around the posts (previous page). This method often is used when there is a considerable drop between levels. It also is a good choice if you want to complete your deck in phases, delaying construction of the lower platform until a later date. See pages 42 to 43.

The support-wall method features a top platform supported by a stud wall that rests on the lower platform, directly over the beam and posts. Unlike the methods listed above, the support-wall method requires that the lower deck platform be built first. This method is a good choice when you want to use decorative wall materials, such as cedar siding, to cover the gap between the two platforms. The support-wall method also works well if you want to complete your deck in phases, delaying construction of the upper level. See pages 44 to 45.

How to Use the Shared Beam Method

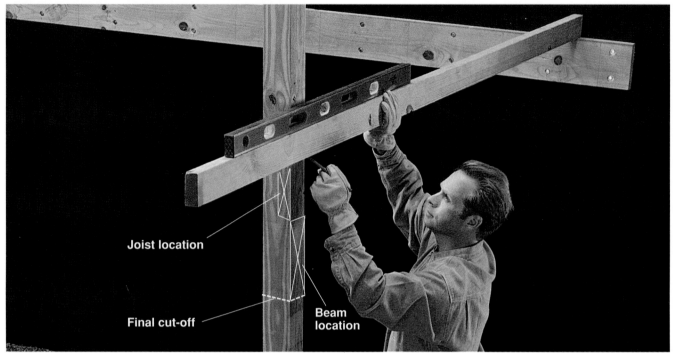

Joist location

Final cut-off

Beam location

1 After laying out and installing the ledger and all posts and footings, mark the posts to indicate where the beam will rest. Use a straight 2 × 4 and level to establish a point level with the top of the ledger, then measure down a distance equal to the height of the joists plus the height of the beam. Cut off the posts at this point, using a reciprocating saw.

2 Position a post-beam cap on each post. Construct a beam from 2 × 10 or 2 × 12 dimension lumber (page 31), then position the beam in the post-beam caps. If the beam is crowned, install it so the crowned side is up; if there is a gap between the middle cap and the beam, shim under the gap. Secure the post-beam caps to the posts and beam with joist-hanger nails.

3 Lay out joist locations for the upper platform on the ledger and on the top of the beam, then use a carpenter's square to transfer joist marks for the lower platform onto the face of the beam. Attach joist hangers at the joist layout lines on the ledger.

4 Measure, cut, and install joists for the upper platform, leaving a 1½" setback to allow for the thickness of the rim joist. At the beam, secure the joists by toenailing with 16d galvanized nails.

5 Attach joist hangers for the lower platform along the face of the beam, using a scrap piece of lumber as a spacer. Cut and install the joists for the lower platform.

6 Cut rim joists for both the upper and lower platforms, and attach them to the ends of the joists by endnailing with 16d nails. Complete the deck, using standard deck-building techniques.

How to Use the Shared Post Method

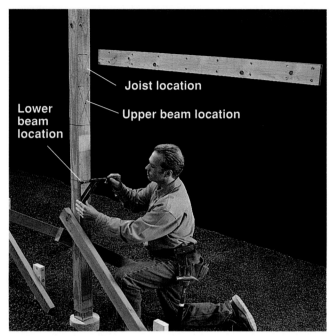

Joist location

Upper beam location

Lower beam location

1 After laying out the deck and installing the ledger and all footings and posts, mark the posts to indicate where both beams will rest. Begin by finding a point level with the top edge of the ledger (page 40), then measure down and mark cutting lines where the bottom of the top beam will rest. For the lower beam, measure down and mark a point on the posts where the top edge of the beam will be positioned.

2 Drill pilot holes, then attach joist ties to the posts with ⅝ × 3" lag screws. The bearing surfaces of the joist ties should be positioned against the line indicating the bottom of the lower beam. Set the beam members in place, then secure with lag screws driven through the joist ties, beam members, and into the posts. Drive additional lag screws through the beam timbers and into the posts, about 1½" from the top edge of the beam.

3 Use a reciprocating saw to cut off the posts at the lines marking the bottom edge of the top beam. Construct the top beam and install it, using post-beam caps (page 31).

4 Lay out and mark the joist locations on the ledger and on the top edges of both the upper and lower beam, using a carpenter's square as a guide.

5 Cut and install the joists for the lower platform, toenailing them to the beams with 16d galvanized nails. Cut rim joists for the lower platform and endnail them to the ends of the joists. Cut and install the joists and rim joist for the upper platform.

6 Attach nailing blocks at the sides of the posts where necessary to provide surfaces for attaching decking boards. Complete the deck, using standard deck-building techniques.

Framing option: If you plan to finish the gap between the upper and lower platform with a decorative wall treatment (pages 90 to 91), install nailing strips between the platforms to provide surfaces for attaching siding materials. Nailing strips and posts should be spaced so the intervals are no more than 16".

How to Use the Support-wall Method

1 Lay out and install the ledger and all posts and footings, then frame the lower platform, using standard deck-building techniques.

2 Use a straight 2 × 4 and level to establish a reference point level with the bottom of the ledger, then find the total height for the support wall by measuring the vertical distance to the top of the lower platform. Cut the wall studs 3" less than this total height, to allow for the thickness of the top and bottom plates.

3 Cut 2 × 4 top and bottom plates to cover the full width of the upper platform, then lay out the stud locations on the plates, 16" on center. Cut studs to length, then assemble the support wall by endnailing the plates to the studs, using galvanized 16d nails.

4 Set a long "sway" brace diagonally across the stud wall, and nail it near one corner only. Square the wall by measuring the diagonals and adjusting until both diagonal measurements are the same. When the wall is square, nail the brace at the other corner, and to each stud. Cut off the ends of the brace flush with the plates.

5 Raise the support wall into position, aligning it with the edge of the beam and the end of the deck. Nail the sole plate to the beam with 16d galvanized nails driven on both sides of each stud.

6 Adjust the wall so it is plumb, then brace it in position by nailing a 1 × 4 across the end stud and outside joist.

7 Lay out joist locations for the upper platform, and install joist hangers on the ledger. Cut joists so they are 1½" shorter than the distance from the ledger to the front edge of the wall. Install the joists by toenailing them to the top plate with 16d nails. Remove the braces.

8 Measure and cut a rim joist, and attach it to the ends of the joists by endnailing with 16d nails. Also toenail the rim joist to the top plate of the support wall. Complete the deck, using standard deck-building techniques. To cover the support wall with siding, see pages 90 to 91.

Building Stairways with Landings

A landing functions essentially as a large step that interrupts a tall stairway. For the builder, the landing provides a convenient spot from which to change the direction of the stairway. For the homeowner, the landing provides a spot to catch your breath momentarily while climbing.

Designing and building a stairway with a landing can be one of the most challenging elements of a deck project. Precision is crucial, since Building Codes have very exact standards for stairway construction. To ensure that the steps for both the top and bottom staircases have the same vertical rise and tread depth, the landing must be set at the right position and height.

Even for professional builders, designing a stairway layout is a process of trial and revision. Begin by creating a preliminary layout that fits your situation, but as you plan and diagram the project, be prepared to revise the layout to satisfy Code requirements and the demands of your building site. Measure your site carefully, and work out all the details on paper before you begin any work. Accuracy and meticulous planning will help ensure that your steps are level and uniform in size.

Remember that any stairway with more than three steps requires a railing (pages 92 to 93).

Building a stairway with a landing is a six-stage project:

- Creating a rough layout (page 50)
- Creating a final layout (page 51)
- Building a stairway landing (pages 51 to 52)
- Laying out stringers (page 53)
- Building the lower staircase (page 54)
- Building the upper staircase (page 55)

Stairway Design Options

Straight layout with no landing may be unavoidable if space on the building site is limited. In this example, the straight stairway layout provides a direct, quick path from a balcony deck to a ground-level platform deck below.

Straight layout with landing is relatively easy to plan and build, but requires more yard space than other stairway designs.

L-shaped layout is used when the building site requires that the stairway change directions.

U-shaped layout is a good choice when space is limited. In the situation shown above, a U-shaped stairway is the most efficient way to connect deck platforms separated by a long vertical rise.

Anatomy of a Stair with Landing

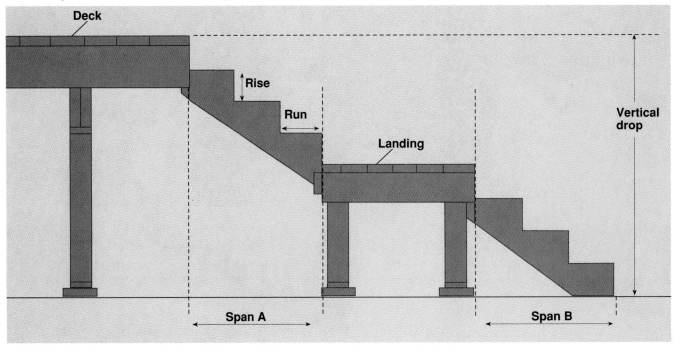

Stairway Basics

The goal of any stairway is to allow people to move easily and safely from one level to another. When designing a deck stairway, the builder must consider the **vertical drop**—the vertical distance from the surface of the deck to the ending point; and the **span**—the horizontal distance from the starting point to the end of the stairway.

During the planning stage, the vertical drop is divided into a series of equal-size steps, called **rises.** Similarly, the horizontal span is divided into a series of equal-size **runs.** On a stairway with a landing, there are two span measurements to consider: the distance from the deck to the edge of the landing, and from the landing to the end point on the ground. In general, the combined horizontal span of the staircases, not counting the landing, should be 40% to 60% more than the total vertical drop.

For safety and comfort, the components of a stairway must be built according to clearly pre-scribed guidelines, as listed at right.

The challenge when planning a stairway is adjusting the preliminary layout and the step dimensions as needed to ensure that the stairway fits the building site and is comfortable to use.

Rises must be no less than 4" and no more than 8" high.

Runs, the horizontal depth of each step, must be at least 9". The number of runs in a staircase is always one less than the number of rises.

Combined sum of the step rise and run should be about 18" to 20". Steps built to this guideline are the most comfortable to use.

Variation between the largest and smallest rise or run measurement can be no more than 3/8".

Stair width must be at least 36", so two people can comfortably pass one another on the stairway.

Stringers should be spaced no more than 36" apart. For added support, a center stringer is recommended for any staircase with more than three steps.

Landings serve as oversized steps; their height must be set as precisely as the risers for the other steps in the stairway. Landings should be at least 36" square, or as wide as the staircase itself. U-shaped stairways should have oversized landings, at least 1 ft. wider than the combined width of the two staircases. Landings very often require reinforcement with diagonal cross braces between the support posts.

Concrete footings should support all stringers resting on the ground.

Construction Details for Stairways

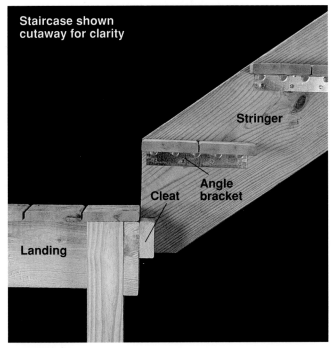

Staircase shown cutaway for clarity

Stringer

Angle bracket

Cleat

Landing

Stringers for the top staircase rest on a 2 × 4 cleat attached to the side of the landing. The stringers are notched to fit around the cleat. On the outside stringers, metal cleats support the treads.

Tread

¾"-thick riser board

Steps may be boxed in the riser boards, and may have treads that overhang the front edge of the step for a more finished look. Treads should overhang the riser boards by no more than 1".

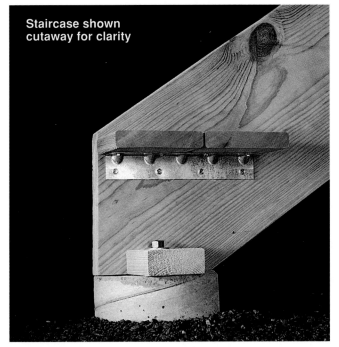

Staircase shown cutaway for clarity

Concrete footings support the stringers for the lower staircase. J-bolts are inserted into the footings while the concrete is still wet. After the footings dry, wooden cleats are attached to the bolt to create surfaces for anchoring the stringers. After the staircase is positioned, the stringers are nailed or screwed to the cleats.

Rim joist

2 × 6 nailer

Center stringers are recommended for any staircase that has more than 3 steps or is more than 36" wide. Center stringers are supported by a 2 × 6 nailer attached to the bottom of the rim joist with metal straps. The bottom edge of the nailer is beveled to match the angle of the stringers. The center stringer is attached by driving deck screws through the back of the nailer and into the stringer.

How to Create a Preliminary Layout

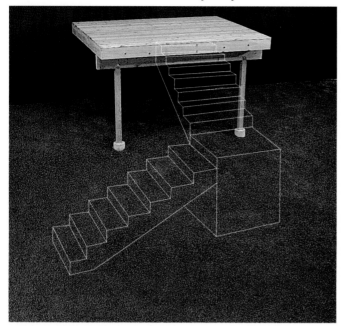

1 Evaluate your building site and try to visualize which stairway design best fits your needs (page 47). When creating a preliminary layout, it is generally best to position the landing so the upper and lower staircases will be of equal length. Select a general design idea.

2 Establish a rough starting point for the stairway on the deck, and an ending point on the ground that conforms with your design. Mark the starting point on the rim joist, and mark the ending point with two stakes, spaced to equal the planned width of your stairway. This is a rough layout only; later calculations will give you the precise measurements.

3 To determine the vertical drop of the stairway, extend a straight 2 × 4 from the starting point on the deck to a spot level with the deck directly over the ending point on the ground. Measure the distance to the ground; this measurement is the total vertical drop. NOTE: If the ending point is more than 10 ft. from the starting point, use a mason's string and line level to establish a reference point from which to measure.

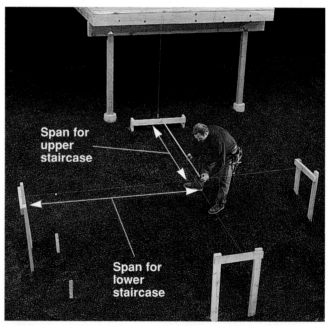

4 Measure the horizontal span for each staircase. First, use batterboards to establish level layout strings representing the edges of the staircases. Find the span for the upper staircase by measuring from a point directly below the edge of the deck out to the edge of the landing. Measure the span for the lower staircase from the landing to the endpoint.

How to Create a Final Layout—an Example

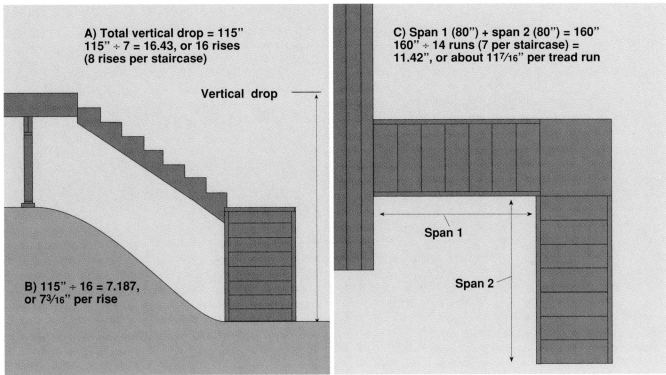

A) Total vertical drop = 115"
115" ÷ 7 = 16.43, or 16 rises
(8 rises per staircase)

Vertical drop

B) 115" ÷ 16 = 7.187,
or 7³⁄₁₆" per rise

C) Span 1 (80") + span 2 (80") = 160"
160" ÷ 14 runs (7 per staircase) =
11.42", or about 11⁷⁄₁₆" per tread run

Span 1

Span 2

1 Find the total number of step rises you will need by dividing the vertical drop by 7, rounding off fractions. (A, example above). Next, determine the exact height for each step rise by dividing the vertical drop by the number of rises (B).

2 Find the horizontal run for each step by adding the spans of both staircases (not including the landing), then dividing by the number of runs (C). Remember that the number of runs in a staircase is always one less than the number of rises.

3 If the layout does not conform with the guidelines on page 48, adjust the stairway starting point, ending point, or landing, then re-calculate the measurements. After finding all dimensions, return to your building site and adjust the layout according to your final plan.

How to Build a Stairway Landing

1 Begin construction by building the landing. On a flat surface, build the landing frame from 2 × 6 lumber. Join the corners with 3" deck screws, then check for square by measuring diagonals. Adjust the frame until the diagonals are equal, then tack a brace across the corners to hold the frame square.

2 Using your plan drawing, find the exact position of the landing on the ground, then set the frame in position and adjust it for level. Drive stakes to mark locations for the landing posts, using a plumb bob as a guide. Install the footings and posts for the landing.

(continued next page)

3 From the top of the deck, measure down a distance equal to the vertical drop for the upper staircase. Attach a 2 × 4 reference board across the deck posts at this height. Position a straightedge on the reference board and against the landing posts so it is level, and mark the posts at this height. Measure down a distance equal to the thickness of the decking boards, and mark reference lines to indicate where the top of the landing frame will rest.

4 Attach the landing frame to the posts at the reference lines. Make sure the landing is level, then secure it with joist ties attached to the posts with 5/8" × 3" lag screws. Cut off the posts flush with the top of the landing frame, using a reciprocating saw.

5 Remove the diagonal braces from the top of the landing frame, then cut and install joists. (For a diagonal decking pattern, space the joists every 12".) Attach the decking boards, and trim them to the edge of the frame.

6 For extra support and to help prevent sway, create permanent cross braces by attaching 2 × 4 boards diagonally from the bottoms of the posts to the inside of the landing frame. Brace at least two sides of the landing. Remove the temporary braces and stakes holding the posts.

Tips for Laying Out Stairway Stringers

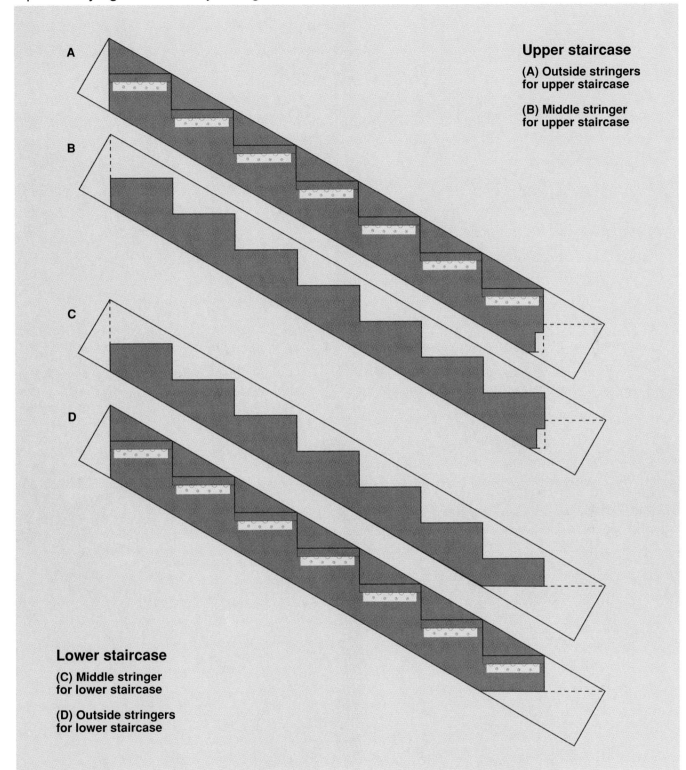

Upper staircase

(A) Outside stringers for upper staircase

(B) Middle stringer for upper staircase

Lower staircase

(C) Middle stringer for lower staircase

(D) Outside stringers for lower staircase

Lay out stringers on 2 × 12 lumber using a carpenter's square. Trim off the waste sections with a circular saw, finishing the notched cuts with a handsaw—in the illustrations above, the waste sections are left unshaded. In standard deck construction, the outside stringers are fitted with metal tread supports that are attached to the inside faces of the stringers. The middle stringer in each flight of stairs is notched to create surfaces that support the stair treads—when cut, these surfaces must align with the tops of the metal tread supports. For the upper staircase stringers, notches are cut at the bottom, front edges to fit over a 2 × 4 cleat that is attached to the landing (see page 49). The top of each notch should lie below the nose of the bottom tread by a distance equal to one rise plus the thickness of a decking board.

How to Build the Lower Staircase

1 Lay out and cut all stringers for both the upper and lower staircases (page 53). For the center stringers only, cut notches where the treads will rest. Start the notches with a circular saw, then finish the cuts with a handsaw. Measure and cut all tread boards.

2 Use ¾"-long lag screws to attach angle brackets to the stringers where the treads will rest, then turn the stringers upside down and attach the treads with lag screws. Gap between tread boards should be no more than ⅜".

3 Dig and pour a concrete footing to support each stringer. Make sure the footings are level and are the proper height to the landing. Install a metal J-bolt in each footing while the concrete is wet, positioning the bolts so they will be offset about 2" from the stringers. After the concrete dries, cut 2 × 4 footing cleats, drill holes in them, and attach them to the J-bolts with nuts (see construction detail, page 49).

4 Attach a 2 × 6 nailer to the landing to support the center stringer (page 49), then set the staircase in place, making sure the outside stringers are flush with the top of the decking. Use corner brackets and joist-hanger nails to anchor the stringers to the rim joist and nailer. Attach the bottoms of the stringers by nailing them to the footing cleats.

How to Build the Upper Staircase

1 Measure and cut a 2 × 4 cleat to match the width of the upper staircase, including the stringers. Use lag screws to attach the cleat to the rim joist on the landing, flush with the tops of the joists. Notch the bottoms of all stringers to fit around the cleat (page 49), and attach angle brackets on the stringers to support the treads.

2 To support the center stringer at the top of the staircase, measure and cut a 2 × 6 nailer equal to the width of the staircase. Attach the nailer to the rim joist with metal straps and screws.

3 Position the stringers so they rest on the landing cleat. Make sure the stringers are level and properly spaced, then toenail the bottoms of the stringers into the cleat, using galvanized 16d nails. At the top of the staircase, use angle brackets to attach the outside stringers to the rim joist and the middle stringer to the nailer.

4 Measure, cut, and position tread boards over the angle brackets, then attach them from below, using ¾"-long lag screws. The gap between tread boards should be no more than ⅜". After completing the stairway, install railings (pages 92 to 93).

Building Decks on Steep Slopes

Positioning and measuring posts on a steep slope is much easier if the deck frame is already in position, resting on temporary supports.

Constructing a deck on a steep slope can be a complicated job if you use standard deck-building techniques. Establishing a layout for posts and footings is difficult on steeply pitched terrain, and construction can be demanding when one end of the deck is far above your head.

Professional deck contractors adapt to steep slope situations by using a temporary post-and-beam support structure, and by slightly altering the construction sequence. Rather than beginning with post-footing layout, experienced builders begin by constructing the outer frame and raising it onto a temporary support structure. Once the elevated frame is in position, the locations of the permanent posts and footings can be determined.

In most instances, you will need helpers when building a deck on a steep slope. To raise and position the deck frame on temporary supports, for example, you will need the help of three or four other people.

On some building sites, a deck may be at a considerable height above the ground. Always exercise caution when working at heights on a ladder or scaffold (page opposite).

The directions on the following pages show the construction of a deck featuring a corner-post design, but the technique can easily be adapted to canti-levered decks.

Safety Tips for Building Decks on Slopes

Stepladders should be used in the open position only if the ground is level. On uneven ground you can use a closed stepladder by building a support ledger from 2 × 6 scraps (inset) and clamping it to a post. Lean the closed ladder against the ledger, and level the base of the ladder, if necessary (below). Never climb onto the top steps of the ladder.

Extension ladders should be leveled and braced. Install sturdy blocking under ladder legs if the ground is uneven or soft, and drive a stake behind each ladder foot to keep it from slipping. Never exceed the weight limit printed on the ladder.

Scaffolding can be leased from rental centers or paint supply stores. When working at heights, scaffolding offers a safer, more stable working surface. Place blocking under the legs of the scaffolding, and level it by screwing the threaded legs in or out.

How to Build a Deck on a Steep Slope

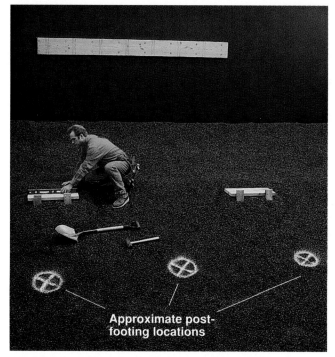

1 After installing the ledger, use spray paint or stakes to mark the approximate locations for the post footings, according to your deck plans. Lay two 2 × 12 scraps on the ground to support temporary posts. Level the scraps, and anchor them with stakes. The bases for the temporary posts should be at least 2 ft. away from post-footing locations.

2 Construct two temporary posts by facenailing pairs of long 2 × 4s together. Erect each post by positioning it on the base and attaching a diagonal 2 × 4 brace. Toenail the post to the base.

3 Attach a second diagonal brace to each post, running at right angles to the first brace. Adjust the posts until they are plumb, then secure them in place by driving stakes into the ground and screwing the diagonal braces to the stakes.

4 Mark a cutoff line on each post by holding a long, straight 2 × 4 against the bottom of the ledger and the face of the post, then marking the post along the bottom edge of the 2 × 4. Cut off the posts at this height, using a reciprocating saw.

5 Construct a temporary support beam at least 2 ft. longer than the width of your deck by facenailing a pair of 2 × 4s together. Center the beam on top of the posts, and toenail it in place.

6 Build the outer frame of your deck according to your construction plans, and attach joist hangers to the inside of the frame, spaced 16" on center. With several helpers, lift the frame onto the temporary sup- ports and carefully move into position against the ledger. NOTE: On very large or high decks, you may need to build the frame piece by piece on top of the temporary support.

(continued next page)

How to Build a Deck on a Steep Slope (continued)

7 Endnail the side joists to the ends of the ledger, then reinforce the joint by installing angle brackets in the inside corners of the frame.

8 Check to make sure the frame is square by measuring the diagonals. If the measurements are not the same, adjust the frame on the temporary beam until it is square. Also check the frame to make sure it is level; if necessary, shim between the temporary beam and the side joists to level the frame. Toenail the frame to the temporary beam.

9 Use a plumb bob suspended from the deck frame to stake the exact locations for post footings on the ground. NOTE: Make sure the footing stakes correspond to the exact center of the posts, as indicated by your deck plans.

10 Dig and pour footings for each post. While the concrete is still wet, insert J-bolts for post anchors, using a plumb bob to ensure that the bolts are at the exact center of the post locations. Let the concrete dry completely before continuing.

11 Check once more to make sure the deck frame is square and level, and adjust if necessary. Attach post anchors to the footings, then measure from the anchors to the bottom edge of the deck beam to determine the length for each post. NOTE: If your deck uses a cantilever design, make sure to allow for the height of the beam when cutting the posts.

12 Cut posts and attach them to the beam and footing with post-beam caps and post anchors (page 31). Brace the posts by attaching 2 × 4 boards diagonally from the bottom of the post to the inside surface of the deck frame (page 52). Remove the temporary supports, then complete the project using standard deck-building techniques.

Joists on a cantilevered deck can be easily marked for angled cuts by snapping a chalk line between two points on adjacent sides of the deck corner. Marking and cutting joists in this fashion is easier than measuring and cutting the joists individually. To help hold them in place while marking, tack a brace across the ends of the joists. Mark joist locations on the brace for reference.

Working with Angles

Decks with geometric shapes and angled sides have much more visual interest than basic square or rectangular decks. Most homes and yards are configured with predictable 90° angles and straight sides, so an angled deck offers a pleasing visual surprise.

Contrary to popular belief, elaborate angled decks are relatively easy to plan and build, if you follow the lead of professional designers. As professionals know, most polygon-shaped decks are nothing more than basic square or rectangular shapes with one or more corners removed. An octagonal island deck, for example, is simply a square with all four corners omitted.

Seen in this light, complicated multilevel decks with many sides become easier to visualize and design.

For visual balance and ease of construction, use 45° angles when designing an angled, geometric deck. In this way, the joinery requires only common cutting angles (90°, 45°, or 22½°), and you can use skewed 45° joist hangers, readily available at home centers. You can, of course, build a deck using irregular angles, but computing the cutting angles on such a deck is much more difficult, and you may need to special-order joist hangers and other hardware.

Design Options for Angled Decks

Cantilever design is the easiest and least expensive to build, since it requires the fewest posts. But the length of the angled side is limited by Code regulations that restrict the amount of joist overhang. And since the joists rest on top of the beam, cantilever designs are not suited for decks with a very low profile. On cantilever designs, the joists along the angled side are beveled at 45° at the ends and are attached to the rim joist by endnailing. See page 65.

Corner-post design is a good choice for large decks with long angled sides. It also works well for low-profile decks, since the joists are mounted to the inside faces of the beams. Many builders use a single beveled post to support the angled corners on this type of deck, but our method calls for two posts and footings at each of these corners, making the design easier to construct and more versatile. On a corner-post deck, the joists on the angled side are square-cut, and are attached to the beam with skewed 45° joist hangers. See page 66.

Multilevel design features an upper platform built using the corner-post method (above), but adds a lower platform (see pages 42 to 43). The lower level is supported by a second angled beam, created by sandwiching timbers around the same posts that support the upper platform. On the lower platform, the joists rest on top of the beam and are beveled on the back ends so they are flush with the edge of the beam. See page 69.

Design & Construction Tips for Angled Decks

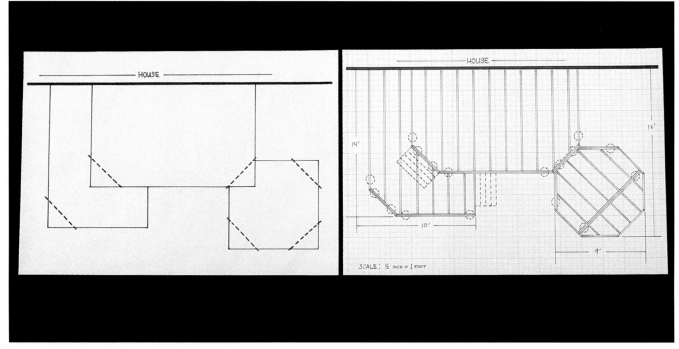

Draw squares and rectangles to create the basic deck platforms, then form angles by eliminating one or more corners. Using this method, you can design an almost infinite variety of single- and multilevel geometric decks. To ensure 45° angles, make sure the sides of the removed corners are the same length.

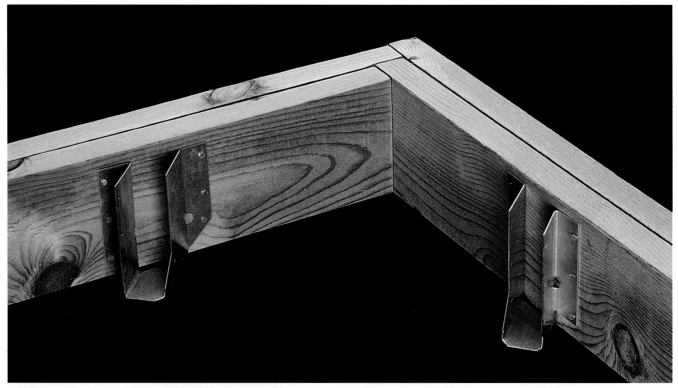

Use skewed 45° joist hangers to install joists when the beams are not parallel to the ledger. When mounted with skewed hangers, joists can be square-cut at the ends. Skewed 45° joist hangers are available at building centers in both left- and right-hand skews. However, if your deck joists angle away from the beam at angles other than 45°, you will need to special-order skewed joist hangers to fit your situation.

How to Build an Angled Deck Using the Cantilever Design

1 Lay out and begin construction using standard deck-building techniques. After installing the joists, mark cutting lines on the angled side by snapping a chalk line across the tops of the joists. Make sure the chalk line is angled 45° to the edge of the deck.

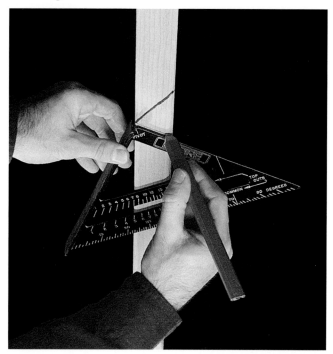

2 At the outside joists, use a speed square to change the 45° chalk line to a line angled at 22½° in the opposite direction. When joined to a rim joist, also cut to 22½°, the corner will form the correct angle.

3 Use a combination square to extend the angle marks down the faces of the joists. Bevel-cut the deck joists with a circular saw, using a clamped board as a guide for the saw foot. Interior joists should be beveled to 45°; outside joists, to 22½°.

4 Cut and install the rim joists. At the angled corners, bevel-cut the ends of the rim joists at 22½°. Endnail the rim joists in place, and reinforce the inside corners with adjustable angle brackets attached with joist-hanger nails (page 69). Finish the deck using standard deck-building techniques.

How to Build an Angled Deck Using the Corner-post Design

1 Use boards to create a rectangular template of the deck. To ensure that the template is square, use the 3-4-5 triangle method: From the corner directly below the ledger, measure 3 ft. along the foundation, and mark a point. Measure out along the template board 4 ft., and mark a second point. Measure diagonally between the two points. This measurement should be 5 ft.; if not, adjust the template to square it.

2 Indicate each angled edge by positioning a board diagonally across the corner of the template. To ensure that the angles measure 45°, make sure the perpendicular legs of the triangle have exactly the same measurement. Nail the boards together where they overlap.

3 Mark locations for post footings with stakes or spray paint. At each 45° corner, mark locations for two posts, positioned about 1 ft. on each side of the corner. Temporarily move the board template, then dig and pour concrete footings.

4 While the concrete is still wet, reposition the template and check to make sure it is square to the ledger. Use a nail to scratch a reference line across the concrete next to the template boards, then insert J-bolts in the wet concrete. Let the concrete dry completely.

5 Attach metal post anchors to the J-bolts, centering them on the reference lines scratched in the concrete. The front and back edges of the anchors should be parallel to the reference line.

6 Measure and cut beam timbers to size. On ends that will form angled corners, use a speed square to mark 22½° angles on the tops of the timbers, then use a combination square to extend cutting lines down the face of the boards. Use a circular saw set for a 22½° bevel to cut off the timbers, then join them together with 16d nails.

7 Set posts into the post anchors, then use a mason's string and line level to mark cutoff lines on the posts at a point level with the bottom of the ledger. Cut off the posts using a reciprocating saw.

Attach post-beam caps to the posts, then set the beams into place. Secure beam corners together with adjustable angle brackets attached to the inside of each corner with joist-hanger nails (page 69).

(continued next page)

How to Build an Angled Deck Using the Corner-post Design (continued)

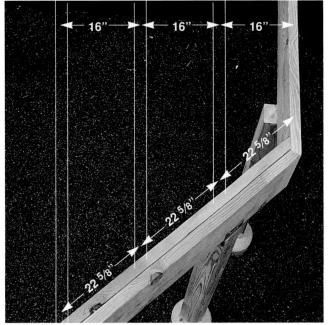

8 Measure and mark joist locations on the ledger and beams. If your joists are spaced 16" on center along the ledger, they will be spaced 22⅝" apart measured along the angled beam. If they are spaced 24" on center at the ledger, the joists will be spaced 33⁵/₁₆" apart along the angled beam.

9 Attach joist hangers at the layout marks on the ledger and beam. Use skewed 45° joist hangers on the angled beam.

10 Cut and install joists, securing them with joist-hanger nails. Joists installed in skewed 45° joist hangers can be square-cut; they need not be beveled to match the angle of the beam. Complete the deck, using standard deck-building techniques.

Corner-post Variation: Adding a Second Platform

1 After installing the beam and joists for the top deck platform, mark the posts to indicate where the beam for the lower platform will be attached. Remember that the joists for the lower deck platform will rest on top of the beam (page 39). To help measure for beam length, clamp scrap pieces of 2 × 4 to the front and back faces of the posts over the layout marks. At corners, the ends of the 2 × 4s should touch.

2 Determine the length for each beam timber by measuring from the point where the 2 × 4 blocks touch. Remember that this measurement represents the short side of the bevel-cut timbers.

3 Lay out and cut beam timbers to length. At angled ends, cut the timbers with a 22½° bevel (page 67). Position and attach the beams to the posts, using 3" lag screws and joist ties. Reinforce angled corners with adjustable angle brackets attached with joist-hanger nails (photo, step 4). Install the remaining posts for the lower platform.

4 Measure and cut joists for the lower platform, attaching them to the beam by toenailing with 16d nails. Where joists rest on the angled beam, position the joists so they overhang the beam, then scribe cutting lines along the back edge of the beam. Bevel-cut the joists to this angle. Cut and install rim joists, then complete the deck using standard deck-building techniques.

Creating Curves

By their nature, curved shapes lend a feeling of tranquility to a landscape. A deck with curved sides tends to encourage quiet relaxation. A curved deck can also provide an effective visual transition between the sharp architectural angles of the house and the more sweeping natural lines of the surrounding landscape.

Curved decks nearly always use a cantilevered design (page 28), in which the curved portion of the deck overhangs a beam that is set back from the edge of the deck. This set-back distance generally should be no more than one-third of the total length of the deck joists, but longer cantilevers are possible if you use a combination of thicker joists, closer joist spacing, and stronger wood species, such as southern yellow pine.

Accurate planning is essential when building a curved deck. Building inspectors carefully scrutinize plans for cantilevered decks, so you will need precisely drawn construction plans and a complete materials list when you apply for a building permit. Detailed plans will also help you define and visualize how you will use the deck, and they can help you save money by determining exact lengths for joists and decking boards.

If your curved deck will be high enough to require a railing, we recommend a design that incorporates a circular curve rather than an elliptical or irregular curve. Adding a curved railing (pages 94 to 97) is much easier if the deck curve is based on a circular shape.

A curved deck is created by cutting joists to match the curved profile, then attaching a curved rim joist, which can be shaped in one of two ways (page opposite). Braces attached to the tops of the joists hold them in place as the rim joist is installed.

Design Options for Curved Decks

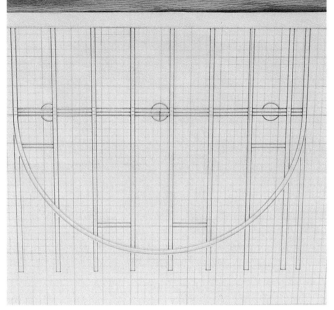

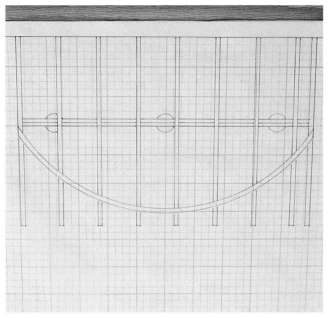

Circular designs are the best choice for curved decks that require railings. However, circular curves require a fairly long cantilever, a limitation that may limit the overall size of your deck. Circular decks are laid out using simple geometry and a long compass tool, called a *trammel,* which you can make yourself. See page 72.

Irregular or elliptical curves should be used only on relatively low decks, since railings are quite difficult to construct for this kind of curve. These designs also work well for large decks, since the amount of overhang on the cantilever is relatively short compared to that for a circular curve. See page 72.

Construction Options

Kerfed rim joist is formed by making a series of thin vertical cuts (kerfs) across the inside face of the board, making it flexible enough to wrap around the curve. A kerfed rim joist made from 2"-thick dimension lumber is sufficiently strong, but if you are kerfing a 1"-thick redwood or cedar fascia board, it should be backed with a laminated rim joist (photo, right). See page 74.

Laminated rim joist is made by bending several layers of flexible ¼" or ⅜"-thick exterior-grade plywood around the curve, joining each layer to the preceding layer with glue and screws. A laminated rim joist can stand alone, or it can provide backing for a more decorative fascia, such as a kerfed redwood or cedar board. See page 75.

How to Lay Out a Curved Deck

1 Install posts and beam for a cantilevered deck. Cut joists slightly longer than their final length, and attach them to the ledger and the beam. Add cross-blocking between the two outside joists to ensure that they remain plumb.

2 Mark the joist spacing on a 1 × 4 brace, and tack it across the tops of the joists at the point where the deck curve will begin. Measure the distance between the inside edges of the outer joists at each end of the beam, then divide this measurement in half to determine the radius of the circular curve. Mark the 1 × 4 brace to indicate the midpoint of the curve.

3 Build a trammel by anchoring one end of a long, straight 1 × 2 to the centerpoint of the curve, using a nail. (If the centerpoint lies between joists, attach a 1 × 4 brace across the joists to provide an anchor.) Measure out along the arm of the trammel a distance equal to the curve radius, and drill a hole. Insert a pencil in the hole, and pivot the trammel around the centerpoint, marking the joists for angled cuts.

VARIATION: For elliptical or irregular curves, temporarily nail vertical anchor boards to the outside joists at the start of the curve. Position a long strip of flexible material, such as hardboard or paneling, inside the anchor boards, then push the strip to create the desired bow. Drive nails into the joists to hold it in position, then scribe cutting lines on the tops of the joists.

4 Use a speed square or protractor to determine the bevel angles you will use to cut the joists. Position the square so the top is aligned with the layout mark on the joist, then find the degree measurement by following the edge of the joist down from the pivot point and reading where it intersects the degree scale on the square.

5 Use a combination square to extend the cutting lines down the front and back faces of the joists. At the outside joists where the curve begins, mark square cutting lines at the point where the circular curve touches the inside edge of the joists.

6 Cut off each joist with a circular saw set to the proper bevel. Clamp a straightedge to the joist to provide a guide for the foot of the saw. On the outside joists where the curve begins, make 90° cuts.

7 Where the bevel angle is beyond the range of your circular saw, use a reciprocating saw to cut off the joists.

How to Construct a Kerfed Rim Joist for a Curved Deck

1 Mark the inside face of the rim joist lumber with a series of parallel lines, 1" apart. Using a circular saw or radial-arm saw set to a blade depth equal to ¾ of the rim joist thickness (1⅛", for 2"-thick lumber), make crosscut kerfs at each line. Soak the rim joist in water for about 2 hours to make it easier to bend.

Blocking

2 Install a cross block between the first two joists on each side of the curve, positioned so half the block is covered by the square-cut outside joist (inset). While it is still damp, attach the rim joist by butting it against the end joist and attaching it to the cross block with 3" deck screws. Bend the rim joist so it is flush against the ends of the joists, and attach with two or three 3" deck screws driven at each joist.

Additional cross block

3 Where butt joints are necessary, mark and cut the rim joist so the joint will fall at the center of a joist. To avoid chipping, cut off the rim joist at one of the saw kerfs.

4 Complete the installation by butting the end of the rim joist against the outside joist and attaching it to the cross block. Use bar clamps to hold the rim joist in position as you screw it to the blocking. NOTE: If the rim joist flattens near the sides of the deck, install additional cross-blocking, cut to the contour of the curve, to hold the rim joist in proper position.

How to Construct a Curved Rim Joist with Laminated Plywood

1 Install blocking between the first two joists on each side of the deck (step 2, previous page). Cut four strips of ¼"-thick exterior plywood the same width as the joists. Butt the first strip against the outside joist and attach it to the blocking with 1½" deck screws. Bend the strip around the joists and attach with deck screws. If necessary, install additional blocking to keep the plywood in the proper curve. If butt joints are necessary, make sure they fall at the center of joists.

2 Attach the remaining strips of plywood one at a time, attaching them to previous layers with 1" deck screws and exterior wood glue. Make sure butt joints are staggered so they do not overlap previous joints. For the last layer, use a finish strip of ⅜" cedar plywood. Where the finish strip butts against the outside joists, bevel-cut the ends at 10° to ensure a tight fit.

How to Install Decking on a Curved Deck

1 Install decking for the square portion of the deck, then test-fit decking boards on the curved portion. If necessary, you can make minor adjustments in the spacing to avoid cutting very narrow decking boards at the end of the curve. When satisfied with the layout, scribe cutting lines on the underside of the decking boards, following the edge of the rim joist.

2 Remove the scribed decking boards, and cut along the cutting lines with a jig saw. Install the decking boards with deck screws, and smooth the cut edges of the decking boards with a belt sander, if necessary.

Framing for Insets

If your planned deck site has a tree, boulder, or other large obstacle, you may be better off building around it rather than removing it. Although framing around a landscape feature makes construction more difficult, the benefits usually make the effort worthwhile. A deck with an attractive tree set into it, for example, is much more appealing than a stark, exposed deck built on a site that has been leveled by a bulldozer.

The same methods used to frame around a preexisting obstacle also can be used to create a decorative or functional inset feature, such as a planter box, child's sandbox, or brick barbecue. On a larger scale, the same framing techniques can be used to enclose a hot tub or above-ground pool.

A framed opening can also provide access to a utility fixture, such as a water faucet, electrical outlet, or central air-conditioning compressor. Covering a framed opening with a removable hatch (page 79) preserves the smooth, finished look of your deck.

Large insets that interrupt joists can compromise the strength of your deck. For this reason, inset openings require modified framing to ensure adequate strength. Double joists on either side of the opening bear the weight of double headers, which in turn support the interrupted joists. Always consult your building inspector for specifics when constructing a deck with a large inset.

Inset framing makes it possible to save mature trees when building a deck. Keeping trees and other landscape features intact helps preserve the value and appearance of your property.

Applications for Framed Insets

Trees inset into a deck should have plenty of room around them to allow for growth and wind sway. In this deck, the planter boxes have been positioned around the inset opening to lend a more natural appearance.

Fire pit can be inset into a deck, if you are careful to use fireproof masonry materials and follow local Code guidelines. This redwood deck has been framed around a brick fire pit that rests on a concrete slab.

Built-in planters can be inset so they are flush with the deck, or they can be built with raised timber sides for more visual impact (above). The same technique can be used to inset a sandbox in a deck.

Hot tubs are often built into a deck. In some situations, the hot tub is supported by the deck structure and is partially enclosed by a secondary platform (pages 80 to 83). Or, the hot tub can be fully inset into the deck, supported by a concrete pad on the ground.

How to Frame for an Inset

1 Modify your deck plan, if necessary, to provide the proper support for the interrupted joists in the inset opening. If the inset will interrupt one or two joists, frame both sides of the opening with double joists. If the opening is larger, you may need to install additional beams and posts around the opening to provide adequate support. Consult your building inspector for specific requirements for your situation.

2 Rough-frame the opening by using double joist hangers to install double joists on each side of the inset, and double headers between these joists. Install the interrupted joists between the double headers and the rim joist and ledger.

3 Where needed, cut and install angled nailing blocks between the joists and headers to provide additional support for the decking boards. When trimmed, decking boards may overhang support members by as much as 4" around an inset opening.

4 Lay the decking boards so the ends overhang the rough opening. Make a cardboard template to draw a cutting line on the deck boards. (When framing for a tree, leave at least 1 ft. on all sides to provide space for growth.) Cut the decking boards along the template line, using a jig saw.

Framing Variations

Inset box can be used as a planter for flowers or herbs. Build the box from ¾"-thick exterior-grade plywood, and attach it to the framing members with deck screws. A deep box can be supported by landscape timbers. Line the inside of the box with layers of building paper, then drill ½"-wide holes in the bottom of the box to provide drainage. To keep soil from washing out through drainage holes, line the box with landscape fabric.

Access hatch made from decking can hide a utility feature, such as a water faucet or air-conditioner compressor. Install cleats along the inside of the framed opening to support the hatch. Construct the hatch from decking boards mounted on a 2 × 4 frame. Finger holes drilled in the hatch make removal easier.

Hot Tub Variation

Hot tub inset completely into a deck requires a concrete pad to support the weight. The surface decking is flush with the lip of the tub, but does not bear any of the tub's weight. For this reason, the deck height must be carefully planned when laying out the posts, beams, and joists.

Framing for a Hot Tub

How to Frame for a Hot Tub

Installing a hot tub into your deck is usually done in one of two ways. If you design your deck at exactly the right height, you can create a full inset by resting the hot tub on a concrete pad and building the deck around it (page 77).

But on a low-profile deck, or a tall deck, the most practical solution is to mount the hot tub on the surface of the deck and build a secondary platform around it, creating a partial inset. As shown on the following pages, the structural design of the deck must be modified to ensure that it can support the added weight of a hot tub filled with water. Make sure your deck plans are approved by the building inspector before you begin work.

Installing a hot tub usually requires the installation of new plumbing and electrical lines. When planning the installation, make sure to consider the location of plumbing pipes, electrical cables, switches, and access panels. For convenience, arrange to have the rough-in work for these utilities done before you install the decking boards.

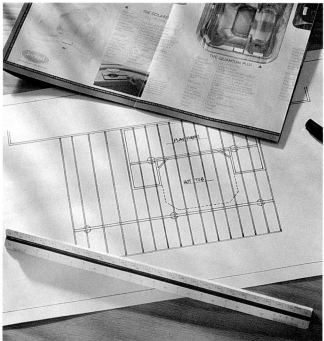

1 Plan posts and beams to support the maximum anticipated load, including the weight of the hot tub filled with water. In most cases, this means altering your deck plan to include extra beams and posts directly under the hot tub.

2 Lay out and install the ledger, footings, posts, and support beams, according to your deck plans. Lay out joist locations on the ledger and beams, and install the joists, following local Code requirements. Many Building Codes require joists spaced no more than 12" on center if the deck will support a hot tub. If your hot tub requires new plumbing or electrical lines, have the preliminary rough-in work done before continuing with deck construction.

3 Install the decking boards, then snap chalk lines to outline the position of the hot tub and the raised platform that will enclose the hot tub.

4 Lay out and cut 2 × 4 sole plates and top plates for the stud walls on the raised platform.

5 Mark stud locations on the top and bottom plates. Studs should be positioned every 16" (measured on center), and at the ends of each plate.

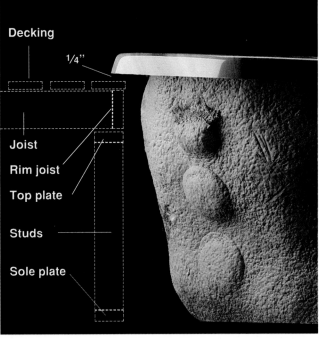

Decking

1/4"

Joist

Rim joist

Top plate

Studs

Sole plate

6 Measure the height of the hot tub to determine the required height of the studs in the platform walls. Remember to include the thickness of both wall plates, the joists that will rest on the walls, and the decking material on the platform. The surface of the finished platform should be ¼" below the lip of the hot tub.

(continued next page)

7 Construct the stud walls by screwing the plates to the studs. Position the walls upright on the deck over the outline marks, and anchor them to the deck with 2½" deck screws.

8 At corners, join the studs together with 3" deck screws. Check the walls for plumb, and brace them in position.

9 Toenail a 2 × 6 rim joist along the back edge of the platform, then cut and install 2 × 6 joists across the top of the stud walls at 16" intervals, toenailing them to the top plates. The ends of the joists should be set back 1½" from the edges of the top plates to allow for the rim joist.

Blocking

10 Cut 2 × 6 rim joists to length, and endnail them to the joists with 16d nails. At angled wall segments, cut diagonal blocking and attach it between the rim joist and adjoining joists with deck screws.

11 Cut decking boards, and attach them to the platform joists with 2½" deck screws. If your hot tub requires cutouts for plumbing or electrical lines, do this work now.

12 Set the hot tub in place, then build 2 × 2 stud walls around the exposed sides of the tub. Measure, cut, and install siding materials on the exposed walls.

13 Build platform steps (page 37) to provide access to the platform, using siding materials to box in the risers. Where required by Code, install railings around the elevated platform (pages 84 to 89).

Railings are required for safety on most decks, but they also contribute to the overall visual appeal. Curved railings like the one shown here are usually built with the vertical baluster style. See pages 94 to 97.

Building Railings

Railings are the crowning touch for a deck project. Required by Code for any deck more than 30" high, railings serve a practical function by making your deck safe. But railings also serve an ornamental function, by helping to create the style and mood of a deck.

There are numerous designs used for deck railings, but most are variations of the styles you will learn how to build on the following pages. The

key to successful railing construction is to have detailed plans. When drawing up railing plans, exercise the same care used when creating your deck plans.

Railing construction is governed by specific Code requirements. See pages 26 to 27 for basic Code guidelines, and consult your local Building Inspector when designing a deck railing.

Railing Options

Vertical baluster railing is a popular style because it complements most house styles. To improve the strength and appearance of the railing, the advanced variation shown here uses a "false mortise" design. The 2 × 2 balusters are mounted on 2 × 2 horizontal rails that slide into mortises notched into the posts. See page 88.

Horizontal railing visually complements modern ranch-style houses with predominantly horizontal lines. For improved strength and a more attractive appearance, the style shown here features 1 × 4 rails set on edge into dadoes cut in the faces of the posts. A cap rail running over all posts and top rails helps unify and strengthen the railing. See page 89.

Wall-style railing is framed with short 2 × 4 stud walls attached flush with the edges of the deck. The stud walls and rim joists are then covered with siding materials, usually chosen to match the siding on the house. A wall-style railing creates a more private space and visually draws the deck into the home, providing a unified appearance. See pages 90 to 91.

Stairway railings are required for any stairway with more than two steps. They are usually designed to match the style used on the deck railing. See pages 92 to 93.

Railing Design Variations

Unique railing patterns give your deck a custom-designed look. The railing shown here was built with 2 × 2s joined with lap joints. You can use any pattern you choose; however, the design must comply with Code requirements. To ensure the safety of children, railings must be constructed so a sphere 4" in diameter cannot fit through any portion of the railing.

Painted railings create an elegant contrast to the natural wood colors found in the decking boards and stairway treads. When painted to match or complement house trim, painted railings help establish consistency of style.

Cables threaded through deck posts create a modern-looking, unobtrusive railing that does not hinder your view. Turnbuckles installed near the edge of the deck can be adjusted to keep the cables taut.

Wall-style railing with horizontal top rails provides a secure barrier for a deck high above the ground, but does not completely obstruct the view.

Railing Construction Tips

Railing posts can be surface-mounted to the edges of rim joists (left), but to improve strength and preserve the smooth lines of the deck, posts can be mounted inside the deck frame (right). Attach the posts with lag screws driven through the deck framing, then cut and endnail extra blocking between joists to reinforce the posts and to provide a nailing surface for attaching decking boards. To ensure sturdiness, posts should be spaced no more than 5 ft. apart.

Specialty railing hardware and wood products make construction easier and can be used to create a railing with a more customized appearance. Common specialty products include rail brackets (A), post caps (B), milled balusters (C), prenotched posts (D), and grippable stairway rails (E).

How to Build a Vertical Baluster Railing

1 Cut 4 × 4 railing posts to size (at least 36", plus the height of the deck rim joists). Lay out and mark partial dadoes 1½" wide and 2½" long where the horizontal 2 × 2 rails will fit. Use a circular saw set to ½" blade depth to make a series of cuts from the edge of the post to the end of layout marks, then use a chisel to clean out the dadoes and square them off. On corner posts, cut dadoes on adjoining sides of the post.

2 Attach the posts inside the rim joists (page 87). To find the length for the rails, measure between the bases of the posts, then add 1" for the ½" dadoes on each post. Measure and cut all balusters. Install the surface boards before continuing with railing construction.

3 Assemble the rails and balusters on a flat surface. Position the balusters at regular intervals (no more than 4" apart), and secure them by driving 2½" deck screws through the rails. A spacing block cut to match the desired gap can make this work easier.

4 Slide the assembled railings into the post dadoes, and toenail them in position with galvanized casing nails. Cut plugs to fit the exposed dadoes, and glue them in place. The resulting joint should resemble a mortise-and-tenon.

5 Measure and cut the 2 × 6 cap rails, then secure them by driving 2" deck screws up through the top rail. At corners, miter-cut the cap rails to form miter joints.

How to Build a Horizontal Railing

1 Cut all 4 × 4 posts to length, then clamp them together to lay out 3½"-wide × ¾"-deep dadoes for the horizontal rails. Cut the dadoes by making a series of parallel cuts, about ¼" apart, between the layout marks. For corner posts, cut dadoes on adjacent faces of the post.

2 Knock out the waste wood between the layout marks, using a hammer, then use a chisel to smooth the bottom of each dado. Attach the posts inside the rim joists (page 87). Install decking before continuing with railing construction.

3 Determine the length of 1 × 4 rails by measuring between the bases of the posts. Cut rails to length, then nail them in place using 8d splitless cedar siding nails. At corners, bevel-cut the ends of the rails to form miter joints. If the rails butt together, the joint should fall at the center of a post.

Cleat

4 Measure and cut 2 × 2 cleats and attach them between the posts, flush with the top rail, using galvanized casing nails. Then, measure and cut cap rails, and position and attach them by driving 2" deck screws up through the cleats. At corners, miter-cut the ends of the cap rails.

How to Build a Wall-style Railing

1 Cut posts to length, then mark the bottoms of the posts for 1½"-deep notches that will allow the posts to fit flush with the outside edges of the rim joists. Make the cross-grain cut first, then set the circular saw to maximum blade depth and make rip cuts from the end of the post to the first cut. Remove the waste wood, and use a chisel, if necessary, to square off the shoulder of the notch. NOTE: A wall-style railing generally requires posts only at the open ends.

2 Attach the posts inside the rim joists with 2½" lag screws, then add blocking between joists to reinforce the posts (page 87). Install decking before continuing with railing construction.

3 Build a 2 × 4 stud wall to match the planned height of your railing. Space studs 16" on center, and attach them by driving deck screws through the top plate and sole plate.

4 Position the stud wall on the deck, flush with the edges of the rim joists, then anchor it by driving 3" deck screws down through the sole plate. At corners, screw the end studs of adjoining walls together. At open ends, screw the end studs to posts.

5 At corners, attach 2 × 4 nailers flush with the inside and outside edges of the top plate and sole plate to provide a nailing surface for attaching trim boards and siding materials.

6 On inside corners, attach a 2 × 2 trim strip, using 10d splitless cedar siding nails. Siding materials will be butted against this trim strip.

7 On outside corners, attach 1 × 4 trim boards on both sides, so one board overlaps the end grain of the other. The trim boards should extend down over the rim joist. Also attach trim boards around posts.

8 Cut and position cap rails on the top rail, then secure them with 2" deck screws driven up through the rail. Railing caps should be mitered at the corners.

9 Attach siding materials to the inside and outside faces of the wall, using splitless cedar siding nails. Snap level chalk lines for reference, and try to match the reveal used on your house siding; the first course should overhang the rim joist slightly. Where joints are necessary, stagger them from course to course so they do not fall on the same studs.

Building Stair Railings

For safety and convenience, any stairway that has more than two risers, or is more than 30" above the ground, should have a railing. The stair railing is generally designed to match the look of the main deck railing.

The dado techniques used to attach deck rails to posts (page 89) are difficult to accomplish with the angled rails on a stairway. Instead, stairway rails can be attached with L-brackets or by toenailing them into the posts.

The sequence shown here demonstrates how to build a horizontal stair railing. A vertical baluster stair railing is built in much the same way, except that it has only two rails, with a series of angle-cut balusters attached between them.

Grippable handrails are required for stairways with more than two risers. The handrail should be shaped so the grippable portion is between 1¼" and 2" in diameter, and should be angled into posts at the ends. The top of the handrail should be 34" to 38" above the stair treads, measured from the nose of a step.

How to Build a Horizontal Stair Railing

1 Use a combination square to mark the face of the top stairway post, where the railings will fit. For most horizontal stairway designs, the top stairway rail should start level with the second deck rail. Mark the other stairway posts at the same level.

2 Position a rail board against the faces of the posts, with the bottom edge against the stringer, then scribe angled cutting lines across the rail along the inside edges of the posts. Cut the rail at these lines, then cut the remaining rails to match.

3 Secure the rails to the posts with galvanized metal L-brackets attached to the inside of the rails.

4 Measure and cut a 2 × 2 cleat, and attach it flush with the top inside edge of the top rail, using 2" deck screws. Anchor the cleat to the posts by toe-nailing with galvanized casing nails.

5 Measure and cut the cap rail to fit over the top rail and cleat. At the bottom of the railing, cut the post at an angle and attach the cap rail so it overhangs the post slightly. Secure the cap rail by driving 2" deck screws up through the cleat.

6 Measure and cut a grippable handrail, attaching it to the posts with mounting brackets. Miter-cut the ends, and create a return back to the post by cutting another mitered section of handrail and nailing it in place between the handrail and post (page opposite).

Building Curved Railings

Laying out and constructing a curved railing requires a basic understanding of geometry and the ability to make detailed drawings using a compass, protractor, and a special measuring tool called a *scale ruler*.

The method for constructing a curved cap rail shown on the following pages works only for symmetrical, circular curves— quarter circles, half circles, or full circles. If your deck has irregular or elliptical curves, creating a cap rail is very difficult. For these curves, it is best to limit the railing design to include only balusters and a laminated top rail.

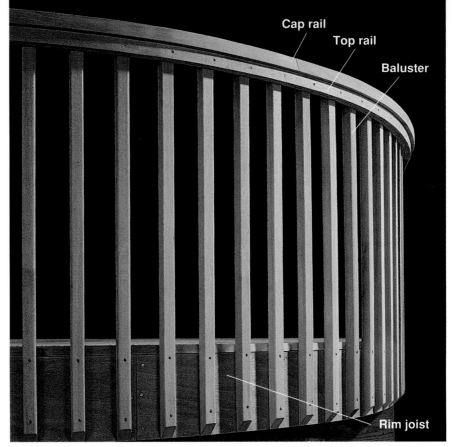

Components of a curved railing include: vertical balusters attached to the curved rim joist, a top rail built from laminated layers of plywood, and a curved cap rail. The cap rail is constructed by laying out mitered sections of 2 × 12 lumber, marking a curved shape, and cutting it out with a jig saw.

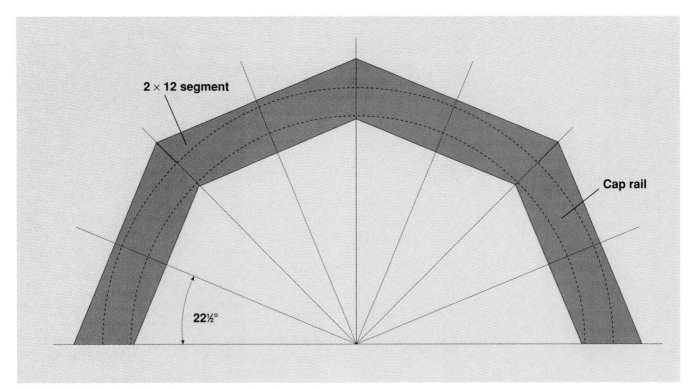

Curved cap rail is created from mitered segments of 2 × 12 lumber. After positioning the 2 × 12 segments end to end, the shape of the 6"-wide cap rail is outlined on the pieces. For a semicircle with a radius of up to 7 ft., four 2 × 12 segments will be needed, with ends mitered at 22½°. For a semicircle with a larger radius, you will need eight segments, with ends mitered at 11¼°.

How to Build a Curved Railing

1 To create a curved top rail, use exterior glue to laminate four 1½"-wide strips of ⅜"-thick cedar plywood together, using the curved rim joist of the deck as a bending form. First, cover the rim joist with kraft paper for protection. Then, begin wrapping strips of plywood around the rim joist. Clamp each strip in position, starting at one end of the curve. The strips should differ in length to ensure that butt joints will be staggered from layer to layer.

2 Continue working your way around the rim joist, toward the other end. Make sure to apply clamps on both sides of the butt joints where plywood strips meet. Cut the last strips slightly overlong, then trim the laminated rail to the correct length after the glue has set. For extra strength, drive 1" deck screws through the rail at 12" intervals after all strips are glued together. Unclamp the rail, and sand the top and bottom edges smooth.

3 Install prenotched 4 × 4 posts (page 87) at the square corners of the deck. Then, cut 2 × 2 balusters to length, beveling the bottom ends at 45°. Attach the balusters to the rim joist with 2½" deck screws, using a spacer to maintain even intervals. Clamp the curved top rail to the tops of the balusters and posts, then attach it with deck screws.

4 After the top rail and balusters are in place, attach 2 × 2 top rails to the balusters in the straight sections of the deck. The ends of the straight top rails should be flush against the ends of the curved top rail. Now, measure the distance between the inside faces of the balusters at each end of the curve. Divide this distance in half to find the required radius for the curved cap rail.

(continued next page)

How to Build a Curved Railing (continued)

5 Using a scale of 1" equals 1 ft., make a diagram of the deck. (A scale ruler makes this job easier.) First, draw the arc of the deck with a compass, using the radius measurement found in step 4. Divide the curved portion of the deck into an even number of equal sections by using a protractor to draw radius lines from the center of the curve. For a semicircular curve, it is usually sufficient to draw eight radius lines, angled at 22½° to one another. (For a deck with a radius of more than 7 ft., you may need to divide the semicircle into 16 portions, with radius lines angled at 11¼°.)

6 From the point where one of the radius lines intersects the curved outline of the deck, use the scale ruler to mark points 5½" above and 5½" below the intersection. From these points, use a protractor to draw perpendicular lines to the adjoining radius lines. The polygon outlined by the perpendicular lines and the adjoining radius lines represents the shape and size for all of the 2 × 12 segments that will be used to construct the cap rail.

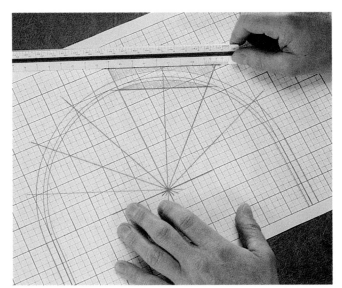

7 Draw a pair of parallel arcs 5½" apart, representing the curved cap railing, inside the outline for the 2 × 12 segments. Shade the portion of the drawing that lies between the straight parallel lines and the two adjacent radius lines. This area represents the shape and size for each of the angled 2 × 12 segments. Measure the angle of the miter at the ends of the board; in this example, the segments are mitered at 22½°.

8 Measure the length of the long edge; this number is the overall length for each of the 2 × 12 segments you will be cutting. Using this highlighted area, determine how many segments you will need to complete the curve. For a semicircular curve with radius up to 7 ft., four segments are required, with ends mitered at 22½°. For curves with a larger radius, you will need eight segments, with ends mitered at 11¼°.

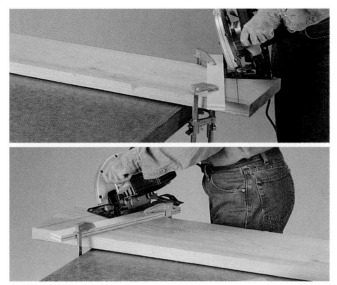

9 Measure and mark 2 × 12 lumber for the cap rail segments, with ends angled inward at 22½° from perpendicular. Set the blade on your circular saw or tablesaw to a 15° bevel, then make compound miter cuts along the marked lines. When cut to compound miters, the segments will form overlapping *scarf* joints that are less likely to reveal gaps between the boards.

10 Arrange the cap rail segments over the curved deck railing, and adjust the pieces, if necessary, so they are centered over the top rail. When you are satisfied with the layout, temporarily attach the segments in place by driving 2" deck screws up through the curved top rail. Measure and install the 2 × 6 cap railing for the straight portion of the railing.

11 Temporarily nail or clamp a long sturdy board between the railings at the start of the curve. Build a long compass, called a *trammel*, by nailing one end of a long 1 × 2 to a 1 ft.-long piece of 1 × 4. Measure from the nail out along the arm of the trammel, and drill holes at the desired radius measurements; for our application, there will be two holes, 5½" apart, representing the width of the finished cap rail. Attach the 1 × 4 base of the trammel to the temporary board so the nail point is at the centerpoint of the deck rail curve, then insert a pencil through one of the holes in the trammel arm. Pivot the arm of the trammel around the cap rail, scribing a cutting line. Move the pencil to the other hole, and scribe a second line.

12 Remove the trammel, and unscrew the cap rail segments. Use a jig saw to cut along the scribed lines, then reposition the curved cap rail pieces over the top rail. Secure the cap rail by applying exterior adhesive to the joints and driving 2½" deck screws up through the top rail. Remove saw marks by belt sanding.

Open space below a deck can be covered with a *skirt* to improve the appearance of the deck. A 2 × 4 framework built between the bottom of the deck and the ground supports the skirting materials. Common choices for skirting materials include lap siding (above) and lattice panels (page 101).

Finishing the Underside of a Deck

The space between the bottom of a deck and the ground often is neglected in the excitement of completing the project. Homeowners who spend thousands of dollars and hundreds of hours building elaborate decks have been known to ignore the underside altogether. Left unfinished, the underside of a deck becomes little more than an eyesore. Too shady for lawn grass, the unattended space quickly becomes a haven for weeds and animal pests.

When finishing the underside of a deck, you have two broad choices: give the space a functional use, or hide it with a decorative screen.

Which option you choose depends largely on the site. If your deck is fairly tall and the ground beneath it is flat, you can turn the space into a functional patio or storage area. But if the area beneath the deck is narrow or steeply sloped, your best option is to make the skirt area more attractive by screening it with landscape plants or wood panels, or by blanketing the soil with a ground cover, such as decorative gravel.

To inhibit weed growth on bare ground under a deck, cover the earth with a layer of landscape fabric before finishing the area.

Options for Finishing the Underside of a Deck

A sheltered, shady patio covered with decking boards or brick pavers can be installed if the ground under the deck is flat. In this example, the expansive area under a large overhead deck is transformed into usable space by laying a ground-level deck platform with built-in benches.

Storage space can be created by walling-in the skirt area with siding materials and installing an access door. This space is ideal for storing yard-care tools and materials, gardening supplies, or children's outdoor toys.

Enclosed porch can be created by laying a water-proof material over the decking surface, finishing the floor area under the deck, then building finished walls around the skirt area, complete with doors and windows. In this example, the area under a small balcony deck has been transformed into a weathertight entry porch.

Ground covers, such as bark chips, gravel, or shrubs, ease the visual transition between the deck and surrounding landscape. Before laying bark or gravel, cover the ground with landscape fabric to inhibit the growth of weeds. For the deck shown above, bark chips and shrubs complement the wood used in the deck and house.

How to Build a Skirt Frame on Uneven Ground

Stud height

1 Cut 2 × 4 sole plates to follow the slope of the ground. Position them directly below the inside edge of the outside deck joist, using a plumb bob as a guide. Lay out stud locations on the outside joist, spaced every 2 ft., and use the plumb bob to mark corresponding locations on the sole plate. Studs will extend from the sole plate to a point about 4" up from the bottom edge of the joists.

2 Mark bevel angles for the bottoms of the studs by holding each stud in a plumb position, with the top against the inside face of the rim joist and the bottom against the inside edge of the sole plate. Scribe a cutting line on the stud, following the edge of the sole plate. Measure the angle with a speed square (page 73), then set the blade of your circular saw to match.

3 Cut studs to length (step 1), then attach the studs to the sole plates with 3" deck screws driven through the bottoms of the sole plates. Attach 1 × 4 braces across the studs near the top to maintain the proper spacing.

4 Position the frame against the inside face of the rim joist. To reduce the likelihood of rot, use temporary 2 × 4 spacers to elevate the frame slightly off the ground. Check for plumb, then attach the frame to the rim joist with 3" deck screws.

5 Secure sole plate joints with galvanized metal plates attached with deck screws.

6 Check to make sure the frame is plumb, then drill ½"-diameter holes through the sole plate between each pair of studs. Drive 1-ft.-long lengths of ½"-diameter steel rebar through the holes and into the ground.

7 Remove the scrap 2 × 4 blocks under the sole plate, then cut skirting materials to fit over the frame. (We used ⅜"-thick cedar lattice panels.) Attach the materials to the frame with 1½" deck screws. Joints between the panels should be aligned over a frame stud.

Call 1-888-330-5600
For Complete Plans

Deck Plans

Simple or complex, a good deck depends on a good plan. To obtain a deck plan that meets your needs, you have several options:

Design it yourself. Use examples and literature to get ideas, then incorporate them into a detailed plan drawing to present to your building official (see page 26).

Hire a designer. Work with a professional landscape designer or residential architect to create a customized deck plan that meets your needs.

Purchase plans. Ready-made deck plans are available for purchase from several sources. Generally, plans include scaled drawings or blueprints of the deck from several perspectives, footing and support information, and materials lists. Many building centers and bookstores carry a selection of these plans.

Complete plans for the deck designs shown on the following pages can be purchased by following the ordering instructions that accompany each plan. Or, simply use these plans to help generate ideas for your own custom design.

Conquering Space

This efficient deck can be tucked into an inside corner space, or built flush against a straight exterior wall. The compact design takes full advantage of usable space. The wraparound steps provide easy access and informal seating for casual get-togethers. A highly practical deck with understated but elegant design features.

Features:

- One level
- Wraparound steps
- Compact design
- Straightforward construction

Overall length: 16 ft.
Overall width: 16 ft.
Area: 232 square ft.

To order complete plans call
1-888-330-5600

Ask for Plan BD-197-01

Cost: $49.95

Framing Plan

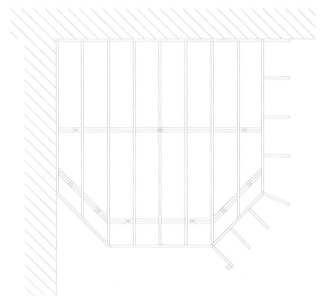

Decking Plan

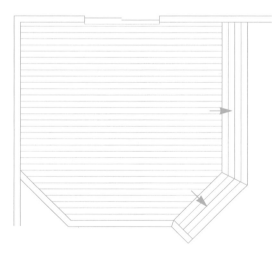

Framing Plan

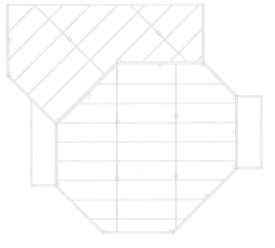

Decking Plan

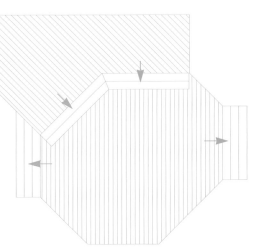

Easy Access Dining

Step down from a compact upper platform to a spacious dining area. With additional steps on each side, the dining area can be approached easily from the ground. Vertical baluster railings surround the angled sides of the deck to make a dramatic design statement.

Features:

- Two levels
- Contrasting decking patterns
- Two access points from ground
- Wide, sweeping steps between upper and lower levels
- Low-profile platform for lower level

Overall length: 24 ft.
Overall width: 24 ft.
Area: 400 square ft. (approx.)

To order complete plans call 1-888-330-5600

Ask for Plan BD-197-02

Cost: $64.95

Lofty Living

Nestled into an outside corner or flat against a wall, this deck will give you a full view of your yard. The basic shape is a simple square with the outside corner removed to create a flat surface for anchoring steps. Decorative railings surround the deck and stairs on all sides.

Features:

- One level
- Central staircase
- Flexible design
- Straightforward construction

Overall length: 16 ft.
Overall width: 16 ft.
Area: 238 square ft. (approx.)

To order complete plans
call 1-888-330-5600

Ask for Plan BD-197-03

Cost: $49.95

**Framing
Plan**

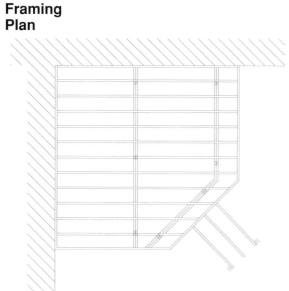

**Decking
Plan**

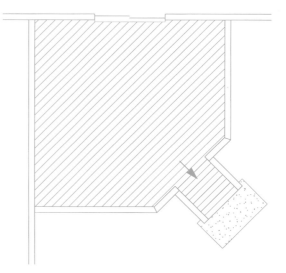

Framing Plan

Decking Plan

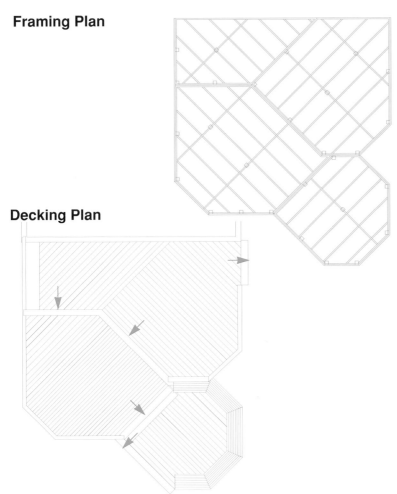

Four Levels of Fun

Your backyard barbecues will succeed on many levels when held on this lovely deck. Four separate platforms create a feeling of intimacy in a deck that provides a substantial amount of surface area. A network of internal posts supports the beams for this deck as they crisscross the deck area.

Features:

- Four levels
- Excellent traffic flow
- Full railings
- Built-in seating
- Large outdoor living area

Overall length: 30 ft.
Overall width: 35 ft.
Area: 858 square ft. (approx.)

To order complete plans
call 1-888-330-5600

Ask for Plan BD-197-04

Cost: $64.95

Social Climber

Three distinct levels blend discreetly into a multifunctional structure in this appealing deck. The rectangular upper platform serves as a suitable perch for viewing the goings-on in the yard and on other deck levels. The irregularly shaped middle and lower levels encourage intimate conversation. The built-in seating that surrounds the lower platform makes a friendly conversation pit.

Features:

•Three levels
•Built-in seating
•Handsome railing
•Interesting angles

Overall length: 19 ft.
Overall width: 14 ft.
Area: 193 square ft. (approx.)

To order complete plans
call 1-888-330-5600

Ask for Plan BD-197-05

Cost: $64.95

Framing Plan

Decking Plan

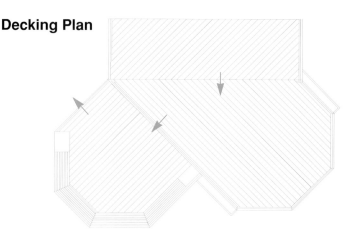

Open Arbor

An expansive two-level deck and an appealing arbor structure combine to create a deck of true distinction. In the shade of the arbor, you can enjoy your multilevel deck even on the hottest summer afternoons. But even without the arbor, this is a very functional, open design that lends itself to just about any outdoor activity.

Features:

- Two levels
- Arbor
- L-shape
- Contemporary, open design

Overall length: 14 ft.
Overall width: 16 ft.
Area: 188 square ft. (approx.)

To order complete plans
call 1-888-330-5600

Ask for Plan BD-197-06

Cost: $49.95

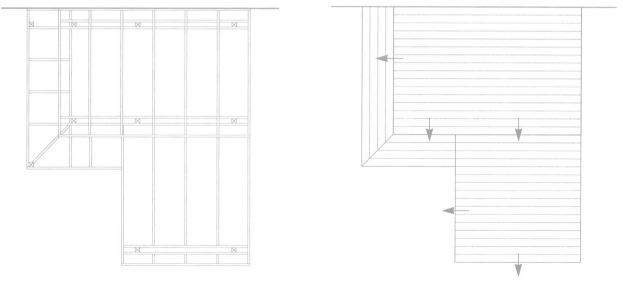

Framing Plan

Decking Plan

The Entertainer

Plenty of square footage spread out over three platforms gives you space for just about all of your outdoor activities. Perfect for the backyard host, this intricate deck gives your home a custom-built feeling. The built-in seating is marked by permanent planters at the ends of each section.

Features:

- Three levels
- Contrasting decking patterns
- Three access points from ground
- Built-in bench seating
- Permanent planters

Overall length: 30 ft.
Overall width: 30 ft.
Area: 475 square ft. (approx.)

To order complete plans
call 1-888-330-5600

Ask for Plan BD-197-07

Cost: $64.95

Framing Plan

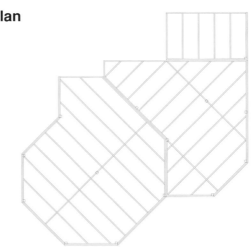

Decking Plan

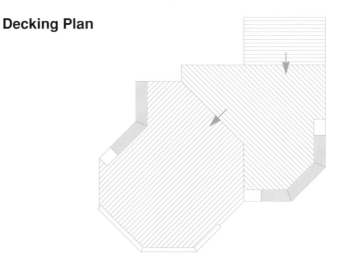

The Processional

Matching staircases on each side of the deck platform keep traffic moving across this unique deck. The decking boards meet in a "bookmatch" pattern to add to the visual effect of the twin staircases. An excellent design for those who make heavy use of their backyard.

Features:

- •One level
- •"Bookmatch" decking pattern
- •Twin staircases
- •Deck and stair railings

Overall length: 16 ft.
Overall width: 12 ft.
Area: 176 square ft. (approx.)

To order complete plans
call 1-888-330-5600

Ask for Plan BD-197-08

Cost: $49.95

**Framing
Plan**

**Decking
Plan**

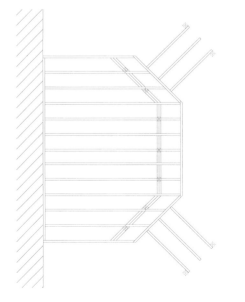

Cascading Cedar

This stunning deck features two platforms, an intriguing staircase and a railing that meanders along the perimeter of the deck. Built from cedar or redwood, it makes a bold statement in a plush setting, but you can use any exterior lumber you choose and still get excellent results. The planters built into the outer stair railing are a truly memorable design feature.

Features:

- Two levels
- Built-in seating
- Winding railing
- Intricate staircases

Overall length: 22 ft.
Overall width: 16 ft.
Area: 298 square ft. (approx.)

To order complete plans
call 1-888-330-5600

Ask for Plan BD-197-09

Cost: $64.95

**Framing
Plan**

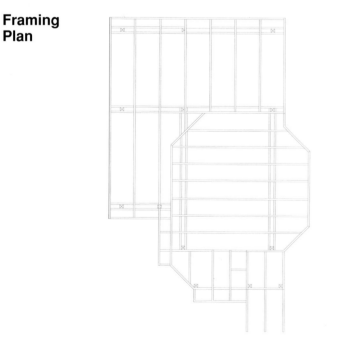

**Decking
Plan**

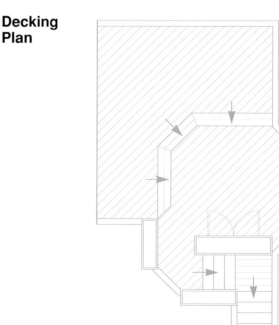

Framing Plan

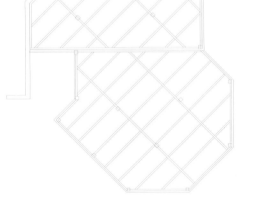

Decking Plan

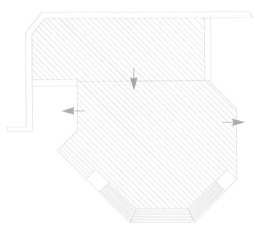

Shady Retreat

A handsome overhead arbor gives this deck a unique decorative touch, while providing relief from direct sunlight. Positioned above the patio doors, the arbor also filters the direct sunlight entering the home, keeping it cooler. A spacious angled deck with built-in benches is attached just a step below the arbor section.

Features:

- Two levels
- Built-in seating
- Overhead arbor
- Large open living area

Overall length: 24 ft.
Overall width: 22 ft.
Area: 305 square ft. (approx.)

To order complete plans
call 1-888-330-5600

Ask for Plan BD-197-10

Cost: $64.95

Rambling Relaxation

Sturdy built-in benches create a sunken conversation pit in this informal multilevel deck. Whether you want to relax in the shade, entertain a large group of friends, or meet in a small gathering for intimate discussions, this multifunctional deck has just the setting you need. The versatile design can be adjusted easily to fit against a flat wall.

Features:

- Three levels
- Built-in seating
- Built-in planters
- Railings galore

Overall length: 30 ft.
Overall width: 28 ft.
Area: 583 square ft. (approx.)

To order complete plans
call 1-888-330-5600

Ask for Plan BD-197-11

Cost: $64.95

Framing Plan

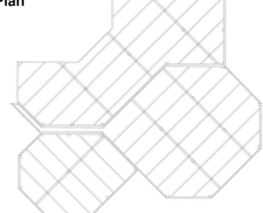

Decking Plan

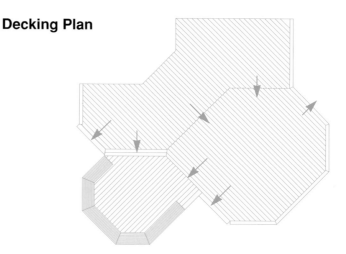

Corner Wraparound

This clever deck wraps around a corner of your house to make full use of space or to extend a view. The sharp angles of the deck contribute to the efficiency of the design, while providing an interesting visual break from the squareness of the house and yard.

Features:

- •One level
- •Staircase parallel to house
- •Covers two sides of house
- •Vertical baluster railing

Overall length: 18 ft.
Overall width: 16 ft.
Area: 230 square ft. (approx.)

To order complete plans
call 1-888-330-5600

Ask for Plan BD-197-12

Cost: $49.95

Framing Plan

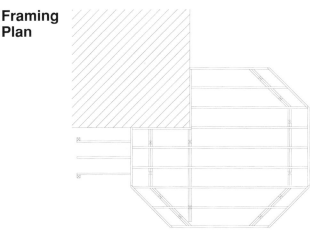

Decking Plan

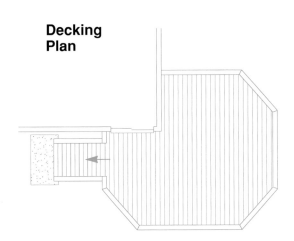

The Wanderer

Framing Plan

This deck has something for everyone. Featuring three large deck platforms laid out in a sprawling pattern, it spreads out over your backyard to make a very dramatic design statement. One of the most unusual deck layouts you will encounter.

Features:

- Three levels
- Built-in seating and planters
- Broad stairs
- Strong sense of movement

Overall length: 28 ft.
Overall width: 24 ft.
Area: 408 square ft. (approx.)

To order complete plans
call 1-888-330-5600

Ask for Plan BD-197-13

Cost: $64.95

Decking Plan

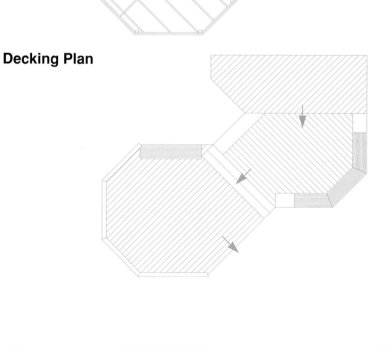

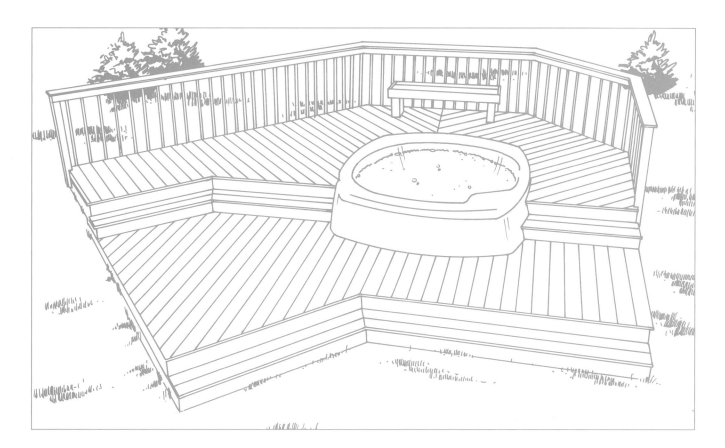

Framing Plan

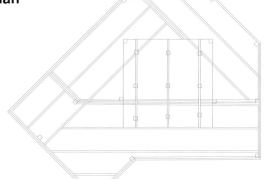

Decking Plan

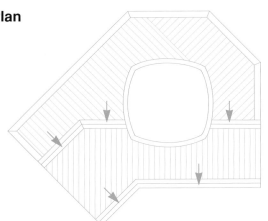

Split-level with Spa

A bold arrangement of angled platforms surrounds an inset hot tub in this deck designed for outdoor recreation. Although the hot tub is the focal point, this deck still contains plenty of space for other outdoor activities.

Features:

- Two levels plus landing
- Inset for hot tub
- Built-in seating
- Built-in planters
- Attractive railing
- Interesting angles

Overall length: 21 ft.
Overall width: 20 ft.
Area: 296 square ft. (approx.)

To order complete plans
call 1-888-330-5600

Ask for Plan BD-197-14

Cost: $64.95

INDEX

Product Information:

For more information on the following products and services contained in this book, call these manufacters:

Metal Connectors
USP Kant-Sag • Silver
    1-800-328-5934

Deck Plans
Homestyles
In addition to deck plans, Homestyles also offers Home Plans. For general information about Home Plans, call
    (612) 338-8155

Deck Materials
California Redwood Association
    (415) 382-0662